New Studies in the Philosophy of Religion

General Editor: W. D. Hudson, Reader in Moral Philosophy,
University of Exeter

This series of monographs includes studies of all the main
problems in the philosophy of religion. It will be of particular
interest to those who study this subject in universities or
colleges. The philosophical problems connected with religious
belief are not, however, a subject of concern only to specialists;
they arise in one form or another for all intelligent men when
confronted by the appeals or the claims of religion.

The general approach of this series is from the standpoint of
contemporary analytical philosophy, and the monographs are
written by a distinguished team of philosophers, all of whom
now teach, or have recently taught, in British or American
universities. Each author has been commissioned to analyse
some aspect of religious belief; to set forth clearly and concisely
the philosophical problems which arise from it; to take into
account the solutions which classical or contemporary philosophers have offered; and to present his own critical assessment
of how religious belief now stands in the light of these problems
and their proposed solutions.

In the main it is theism with which these monographs deal
because that is the type of religious belief with which readers
are most likely to be familiar, but other forms of religion are not
ignored. Some of the authors are religious believers and some
are not, but it is not their primary aim to write polemically,
much less dogmatically, for or against religion. Rather, they set
themselves to clarify the nature of religious belief in the light of
modern philosophy by bringing into focus the questions about
it which a reasonable man as such has to ask. How is talk of
God like, and how unlike, other universes of discourse in which
men engage, such as science, art or morality? Is this talk of God
self-consistent? Does it accord with other rational beliefs which
we hold about man or the world which he inhabits? It is
questions such as these which this series will help the reader to
answer for himself.

New Studies in the Philosophy of Religion

IN THE SAME SERIES

Published

The Concept of Miracle

RICHARD SWINBURNE

Senior Lecturer in Philosophy, University of Hull

Macmillan
St Martin's Press

First published 1970 by
MACMILLAN AND CO LTD
London and Basingstoke
Associated companies in New York Toronto
Dublin Melbourne Johannesburg and Madras

Library of Congress catalog card no. 72-124956

SBN 333 10503 6

Printed in Great Britain by
ROBERT MACLEHOSE AND CO LTD
The University Press, Glasgow

Contents

Editor's Preface

This series of 'New Studies in the Philosophy of Religion' is designed to provide contemporary treatments of the main problems in the philosophy of religion. The authors are all philosophers who teach, or have taught, philosophy in the universities of Great Britain or the United States. Some of them are religious believers and some are not. Their main purpose, however, is not to write polemically for or against religious belief. It is rather to analyse certain main aspects of belief, in particular of theism since that is the type of religion with which most readers of this series are likely to be familiar, and to bring to light the philosophical problems which arise in connexion with each aspect of it. They examine critically what other philosophers, both classical and contemporary, have said about these problems and then offer their own opinions. The series as a whole will present a clear and comprehensive picture of how religion appears from the point of view of modern analytical philosophy.

In this monograph Mr Swinburne deals with the philosophical questions which arise concerning miracles. Do the latter occur? It is obviously essential to decide first of all what they are and there is some variety of opinion about that even amongst believers. Once we get the concept, or concepts, of miracle clear the question of the internal coherence of this concept, or these concepts, arises. Is it logically impossible for miracles to occur or at least for us ever to know that one has occurred? The author copes with such questions clearly and concisely. His treatment will be of great value to those reading philosophy at university and his line of argument will interest professional philosophers. To a wider circle of readers, however, this monograph will be of no less value and interest. Most intelligent men find it necessary to make up their minds about religion and this monograph will help to put them in the picture so far as one aspect of what they are making up their minds about is concerned.

University of Exeter   W. D. Hudson

Preface

Some of the material used in this book appeared as an article in the *Philosophical Quarterly* ('Miracles', xviii (1968) 320–8). I am grateful to the editor of that journal for permission to use the material here.

I am most grateful to all who by their helpful criticism made this book less inadequate than it would otherwise have been: to Paul Gilbert, Edgar Page, Christopher Williams, and the general editor of the series, Dr W. D. Hudson, who read through the whole of a previous draft; to all who commented on a paper containing much of the material of Chapter 4, which was read at various universities; and to my wife for correcting typescript and proofs.

Richard Swinburne

Why science cant answ all

1) It is limited in knowledge
2) It cant tell why
3) It cant disprove God
4)

1 Senses of 'Miracle'

There are many different senses of the English word 'miracle' (and of words normally so translated into English). In this chapter I shall distinguish these different senses, and show how they are related. I shall end by justifying my taking a particular sense of the word for subsequent philosophical analysis. I shall in subsequent chapters consider in detail what it means to say that in this sense a miracle occurred, and what would be evidence that it did. My analysis of this sense should indicate the way in which claims about miracles in other senses of the word are to be analysed, and so supported or refuted.

A wide definition of 'miracle'

To start with we may say very generally that a miracle is an event of an extraordinary kind, brought about by a god, and of religious significance. But some of the terms in this definition can be interpreted in various ways, which we must now distinguish. Further, 'miracle' is sometimes used in a wider or a narrower sense than any of the senses which result from giving a precise meaning to some of the vague terms of this initial definition. These we must clarify.

'An event of an extraordinary kind'

What is to count as 'of an extraordinary kind' depends on what is one's understanding of what happens ordinarily. Thus, on the view of Aristotle inherited by most medieval thinkers, each object belonged to a kind, and objects of each kind had natures specific to objects of that kind. An object's nature determined how it behaved naturally – that is, when not acted upon by another object. Thus it belonged to the nature of a plant to take in nourishment, grow and subsequently decay, and its doing these things was natural behaviour for it. Other objects,

1

however, in virtue of their natures could make an object do what it would not do naturally (when that behaviour of the latter object was it moving, that motion was said to be violent motion). A plant could not by its nature move across the Earth, but a man could carry it across the Earth, thereby subjecting it to violent motion. A man's nature was such that he had the power of producing such motion in the plant. So the occurrences in the world, that is, the changes of state of objects, were either occurrences which were natural behaviour of the objects concerned or were produced by other objects who by nature had the power to produce such occurrences.

St Thomas Aquinas (c. 1225–74) claimed that to be a miracle an event had to be such as to be beyond the natural power of any created thing to produce (see his [2] ch. 102). (1) It was in consequence of this understanding of 'extraordinary' that Aquinas held that God, as alone un-created, could alone work miracles. Others however, and especially Pope Benedict XIV (1675–1758), whose work *De Miraculis* forms a standard statement of Roman Catholic doctrine, more naturally allow that something is a miracle whose production exceeds 'the power of visible and corporeal nature only' ([3] 1.1.12). Hence on Benedict's view angels could work miracles. He further held that men could work miracles if they were for an instant given (by an agent able to bestow such powers) powers beyond their nature.

However, talk about objects having natures in virtue of which they have certain powers to act is talk that belongs to ancient rather than modern science. Since the seventeenth century we have come to think of the behaviour of things as governed not by their nature or by other objects in virtue of their nature but by laws of nature, or natural laws, which declare which events must or must probably follow other events. (This new way of talking is not one forced on men by any new scientific discovery but simply a different and perhaps more convenient way of setting forth our knowledge of the behaviour of things.)

Natural laws may be universal or statistical in form. Universal laws are of the form 'so-and-sos always do (or are) such-and-such'; statistical laws are of the form 'n% so-and-sos do (or are) such-and-such'. Universal laws state what must happen, statistical laws state what must probably happen, in a particular

2

case. Paradigm examples of universal laws are Newton's three laws of motion and his law of gravitation, which together state how bodies of different masses having certain initial arrangement and velocity subsequently have certain other arrangements and velocities. Since the eighteenth century many men, and especially scientists, have believed that natural laws governed all events of all kinds, determining from the preceding state of the Universe what its subsequent state was to be. From the eighteenth to the beginning of the twentieth century most men believed that all natural laws were universal. Yet since the development of Quantum Theory in this century many scientists have come to hold that the fundamental natural laws are statistical. These are the laws governing the behaviour of the fundamental particles, such as photons, electrons and mesons, out of which the ordinary familiar objects which surround us are composed. The laws state, for example, that in the long run a certain proportion of photons reaching a potential barrier will pass through it and a certain proportion will be reflected, but one can only deduce therefrom a probability of an individual photon passing the barrier. However, although the probability of some small-scale event is often not especially close to one or zero, probabilities on the small scale often produce near-certainties on the large scale. Although one is far from certain what an individual fundamental particle will do, idiosyncrasies cancel out, and one can be pretty near certain to within a minute margin of error what a large number of such particles will do – which is why the behaviour of ordinary sized objects is in general so consistent (just as it follows that if it is equally probable that a coin will fall heads or tails on any one occasion, then in a million throws very nearly half of the throws will be heads and very nearly half will be tails).

Given talk of natural laws, an event which goes against them or 'violates' them would seem to be an event 'of an extraordinary kind' (this notion of violation will be examined in more detail in Chapter 3). If the laws are universal such an event would be an event whose non-occurrence the laws predicted. If the laws are statistical, an event whose occurrence is rendered highly improbable by them would seem to be an event of 'an extraordinary kind'. These seem to me to be the most natural modern equivalents of an event whose production exceeds the power of visible and corporeal nature. Many have

3

certainly understood an event of this kind to be well on the way to being a miracle.

However, there are events of an extraordinary kind which occur in perfect accordance with natural laws, which many might want to consider as candidates for being miracles. These are extraordinary coincidences. Even given the truth of determinism (that universal natural laws govern all occurrences, and that there are no exceptions to their operation) what happens is not solely a function of which laws operate. Laws state the subsequent effect of certain initial conditions, and what happens is a function as much of the initial conditions as of the laws. The state of the world today, given determinism, is a consequence of its state yesterday, and its state yesterday a consequence of its state the day before, and so on. (If there was an initial moment of the Universe, then its subsequent state is, given the laws, a consequence of its initial state.) Now in any period of history events of certain kinds are very frequent, and events of other kinds very rare, and which are frequent and which are rare is, for any given set of natural laws, a consequence of a past state of the Universe (which will not itself have been determined solely by the laws, but by yet earlier states, if such there were). While the laws alone determine which event succeeds which, their coincidences (which event happens at the same time as which other event) depend also on initial states. Some coincidences will be normal, some abnormal or extraordinary. Some philosophers and theologians have wanted to allow the extraordinary coincidence as an event of an extraordinary kind which was a candidate for being a miracle, and ordinary talk would seem to allow this usage.

Professor R. F. Holland gives the following example of a coincidence which would be a candidate for being a miracle:

A child riding his toy motor-car strays on to an unguarded railway crossing near his house and a wheel of his car gets stuck down the side of one of the rails. An express train is due to pass with the signals in its favour and a curve in the track makes it impossible for the driver to stop his train in time to avoid any obstruction he might encounter on the crossing. The mother coming out of the house to look for her child sees him on the crossing and hears the train approaching. She runs forward shouting and waving. The little boy remains

4

seated in his car looking downward, engrossed in the task of pedalling it free. The brakes of the train are applied and it comes to rest a few feet from the child. The mother thanks God for the miracle; which she never ceases to think of as such although, as she in due course learns, there was nothing super-natural about the manner in which the brakes of the train came to be applied. The driver had fainted, for a reason that had nothing to do with the presence of the child on the line, and the brakes were applied automatically as his hand ceased to exert pressure on the control lever. ([18] p. 43)

So then in these various ways an event may be an event 'of an extraordinary kind' and so a candidate for being a miracle. This requirement may however on occasion become weakened into the requirement that to be a miracle an event appear to be of an extraordinary kind, not necessarily actually be so.

This weakening is particularly likely to occur for events whose actual or apparent extraordinary character arises because their production exceeds the power of visible or corporeal nature, or, in modern terms, because they violate the laws of nature, and for the following reason. On the Aristotelian view it was a matter for philosophico-scientific inquiry to ascertain what was the nature of an object, and so to ascertain what powers did not by nature belong to an object, and in the absence of scientific knowledge mistakes would be made about the latter. Aquinas comments that 'when any finite power produces the proper effect to which it is determined, this is not a miracle, though it may be a matter of wonder for some person who does not understand that power. For example, it may seem astonish-ing to ignorant people that a magnet attracts iron' ([2] 102.1). The ignorant, Aquinas is saying, might believe that attracting iron was beyond the natural powers of the magnet and so be disposed to call a case of attraction a miracle, but they would be mistaken as a result of their lack of scientific knowledge. Likewise with the modern view it is a matter of scientific investigation to ascertain what are the laws of nature, and we may at any time be mistaken about this and so about what is a violation of a natural law. But it is difficult to ascertain for certain when, objectively, the production of some event is beyond the natural powers of the objects involved in it, or its occurrence is an exception to (or highly improbable on)

5

natural laws. Hence the subjective sense appears. In this sense some event is a miracle if it appears to be a violation of natural laws, whether or not it is what it appears, given, perhaps, that other conditions are also fulfilled.

Although the term is occasionally used in this subjective sense, I do not think that this use is in fact at all common. For normally if something previously believed to be a violation of natural laws and for that reason a miracle is shown in fact to be in accord with natural laws, we are apt to say that it was not a miracle at all after all, not that it is now no longer a miracle.

'An event brought about by a god'

The second condition stated in my original definition was that to be a miracle an event must be brought about by a god. I understand by a god a non-embodied rational agent of great power. By the agent being 'non-embodied' I mean that (except perhaps temporarily and by his own choice) he has no body; there is no one material object, occurrences affecting which he feels and which he has particularly under his control, to be distinguished from other material objects of which this is not true. By a rational agent I mean a being who can reason, choose, decide, intend, has likes and dislikes, is capable of moral or immoral action. By the agent being of great power I mean that he can produce effects in the world far beyond the powers of men to produce.

This second condition can be made more tight or more loose. On a tighter definition an event would only be a miracle if brought about by God, not by any god. By God I mean the God of the Christians, Jews and Moslems. (Since the defining properties which Christianity, Judaism and Islam ascribe to 'God' are very similar – e.g. omnipotence, omniscience, all-goodness etc. – it is natural to say that Christians, Jews and Moslems worship the same God. They do of course hold that different further properties belong to him apart from the defining properties, e.g. Christians, unlike Moselms, believe that he is three 'persons' in one 'substance', and that he redeemed the world through Christ. But these seem to be properties ascribed to a being defined in other ways.)

If we do define miracle in this way then it is of course logically necessary (that is, necessary in virtue of the meaning of the terms used) that there can be no miracles, unless the Christian

6

God exists. Thus there cannot be miracles which are evidence for his existence because accepting a description of an event as a miracle commits a man to accept the existence of God. Yet Christians often do want to talk of miracles as evidence for the existence of God. Further, in discussion with others they may admit that miracles occur in the context of other religions, and consider the possibility that beings other than God have brought these about. Yet this is a possibility that could not even be raised if it was part of the meaning of 'miracle' that it was an event brought about by God. For these reasons to require that a miracle be an event brought about by God seems to place a restriction on the use of the term not justified in general by practice. However, as we noted earlier, Aquinas wanted to define 'miracle' in such a way that God alone could work miracles.

The second condition could be made looser by allowing any agent, not necessarily a god, to work miracles. It does not seem obviously self-contradictory to suppose that some embodied rational agent such as a man worked a miracle. True, in many biblical 'miracle' stories and subsequent 'miracle' stories from Christian history the alleged agent of the miracle is a god, that is God or an angel (and on the Christian understanding of Jesus his 'miracles' might be said to be wrought by a god, that is, God). But there are other stories not unnaturally described as 'miracle' stories in which the alleged agent of the miracle is unquestionably a man – see e.g. Acts 3:1–9, where Peter heals a lame man.

Benedict would allow that any one who works an effect 'beyond the power of visible or corporeal nature' works (subject to a further requirement to be discussed) a miracle. He presents two views – one that creatures are only the 'moral' causes of miracles (viz. the cause of miracles only in virtue of having asked God to bring them about), and the other that creatures are sometimes the 'physical' cause of miracles – and though regarding the issue as somewhat trivial, he seems to prefer the latter view ([3] 1.2). This means that not merely can any god (e.g. an angel) work a miracle, but also a man can do so.

'An event of religious significance'

The third requirement in my earlier definition for an event being a miracle is that it should have religious significance. If a god intervened in the natural order to make a feather land here rather than there for no deep ultimate purpose, or to upset a child's box of toys just for spite, these events would not naturally be described as miracles. To be a miracle an event must contribute significantly towards a holy divine purpose for the world.

On a wide understanding of 'religious significance' an event will have religious significance if it is a good event and a contribution to or foretaste of the ultimate destiny of the world. Thus the healing of a sick person will, on the Christian view, be of religious significance, since the world's ultimate destiny is, on the Christian view, a state where evil, including sickness, is no more. Or the train stopping, in Holland's example quoted earlier, will be of religious significance on the Christian view since a separation by death of mother and child is an evil to be abolished in the last state of the world.

But narrower views of religious significance are possible. For Benedict XIV it is required of miracles 'that they serve to confirm The Catholic Faith, or to demonstrate the sanctity of some man' ([3] 1.4.6). One way in which an extraordinary event could 'confirm' a doctrine would be if it occurred in answer to prayer asking for confirmation of the doctrine as, if it occurred, did Elijah's purported miracle on Mount Carmel (1 Kings 18).

Elijah challenged the prophets of Baal, 'Call ye on the name of your god, and I will call on the name of the Lord: and the God that answereth by fire let him be God.' The prayer of the prophets of Baal got no response, but in answer to Elijah's prayer 'the fire of the Lord fell, and consumed the burnt offering, and the wood, and the stones, and the dust', soaked in water, 'and licked up the water that was in the trench'. Another way in which an extraordinary event could confirm a doctrine could be by symbolising it. If Jesus fed the five thousand in the wilderness with the five loaves and two fishes (see e.g. John 6:1–14), he was repeating on a larger scale an event believed to have been performed by Elisha (2 Kings 4:42 ff.) and thus, on the Jewish understanding, symbolising his being a new and greater Elisha.

So then religious significance can be understood in a wider or narrower sense. But in order to be a miracle, an event must surely have religious significance in some sense. Extraordinary

8

events lacking religious significance are more appropriately characterised as magical or psychic phenomena rather than as miracles. It was for this reason that Benedict denied that demons could work miracles:

> If someone inferred that demons by their natural power can work miracles he would be mistaken. . . . As Estius correctly observes '. . . the demons do not teach any truth which they might want to confirm by miracle; nor do they work any miracles by themselves or through others, in order to testify to their sanctity which they do not have. Either one of these two intentions seems to be necessary to say that someone works a miracle.' ([3] 1.3.15)

It is for the reason that miracles must have religious significance that many ancient writers on miracles have written that a miracle is not an event contrary to nature, but an event beyond nature. The point of this remark is that while an event which is a miracle is not in accordance with the nature of the objects involved in it, it is nevertheless in accordance with the divinely ordained natural order as a whole. It is indeed, Aquinas would argue, contrary to the nature of the sea that it 'open up and offer a way through which people may pass', but its doing so at the time of the Israelite exodus from Egypt was part of the divine plan for the human race, and so in a sense very much a natural event. Miracles are events with a point in the overall scheme of things and so in a sense very much regular.

For a few modern writers any event of great religious significance is, as such, a miracle. It is for them not necessary that it be an event of an extraordinary kind brought about by a god or a man using abnormal powers (in the senses earlier described). A definition of this kind is offered by the influential Protestant theologian Paul Tillich (1886–1965). He suggested that 'a genuine miracle is first of all an event which is astonishing, unusual, shaking, without contradicting the rational structure of reality. In the second place it is an event which points to the mystery of being, expressing its relation to us in a definite way. In the third place it is an occurrence which is received as a sign-event in an ecstatic experience. Only if these conditions are fulfilled can one speak of a genuine miracle' ([9] p. 130). But although one can of course use the word 'miracle' in such a sense, if one chooses, it seems to be not the normal sense, and to take over a job often done previously by the word 'sign' (or words so translated into English). When Ezekiel joined two sticks (Ezekiel 37:15–28) to show that God would unite into one people the tribes of Israel and Judah, there was nothing above nature in his physical movements, although his action had great religious significance. On a Tillichian definition Ezekiel would have done a miracle, but it seems more natural to say that he did a sign, although there was nothing miraculous in what he did.

As well as being used in the ways described above, the word 'miracle' is sometimes used by people who do not wish to make any religious point by their use of it. 'It was a miracle' may sometimes mean simply that the event referred to was highly unexpected and highly desirable. This use of 'miracle' seems very much a derivative use. As it is of no interest for the philosophy of religion, I shall not be further concerned with it.

On our initial definition, a miracle was an event of an extraordinary kind, brought about by a god, and of religious significance. We have seen how the phrases in this definition may be taken more narrowly or more widely. Thereby different senses of 'miracle' result. We have seen how one or two senses of 'miracle' have been used, other than those which result from a widening or narrowing of the above definition. We have seen that these cannot in general be regarded as normal uses of the term 'miracle', though we have admitted that it does seem natural to allow that the agent of a miracle could be a man.

Philosophical problems about miracles

The concepts of 'extraordinary coincidence' or 'religious significance' do not seem to raise any philosophical problems peculiar to the topic of miracles. The notion of a coincidence is perfectly comprehensible, and, given a religious system established on good grounds, the concept of religious significance seems perfectly comprehensible and applicable. (To examine the grounds for postulating such a system would be to go beyond the narrow confines set for this book.) The main philosophical problems arise with the other concepts to which we have referred. Hence for the rest of this book, unless explicitly stated otherwise, I shall use a more precise definition of miracle with the application of which all the philosophical problems peculiar to the topic of miracle arise. I shall in these chapters understand by a miracle *a violation of a law of nature by a god*. This definition is in effect the same as that given by the Scottish philosopher David Hume (1711–76). Hume wrote that 'a miracle may be accurately defined, a transgression of a law of nature by a particular volition of the Deity, or by the interposition of some invisible agent' ([10] p. 115, n.1). I start from Hume because Hume put forward the philosophical thesis that the evidence would almost inevitably be against the occurrence of any purported miracle, and his arguments have carried very considerable weight in the English philosophical tradition. In Chapter 2 I will expound Hume's thesis and its development by his philosophical successors. In Chapter 3 I will consider what is meant by a violation of a law of nature, and in Chapter 4 I will consider what historical evidence there could be for the occurrence of a particular event which, if it occurred, would have been a violation of a law of nature. In Chapter 5 I will consider what historical evidence there could be that a god was responsible for the violation. In Chapter 6 I will consider evidence, other than the historical and scientific evidence about violations, relevant to showing the occurrence of miracles on the narrow definition being considered. Towards the end of the book I shall indicate briefly how historical and other evidence could count for or against the occurrence of other miracles in other senses. At the end of the book a bibliography is provided of the discussions of these issues, which are of the greatest historical importance.

2 The Humean Tradition

So then, following Hume, let us for the moment understand by a miracle a violation of a law of nature by a god. Hume's discussion of miracles is contained in section x ('Of Miracles') of his *Enquiry Concerning Human Understanding* [11]. Part 1 of section x is devoted to showing on philosophical grounds that the evidence against the occurrence of any purported miracle is normally liable to be extremely strong and to outweigh by far the evidence in favour of the occurrence. Part 2 is devoted to showing that, although in theory the evidence in favour of the occurrence of a miracle could on occasion outweigh the evidence against it, in practice this never happens.

Hume's main argument

The argument of part 1 is as follows. When he is conducting any enquiry, and, in particular, any historical inquiry 'a wise man . . . proportions his belief to the evidence' ([11] p. 110). If it be claimed that some particular event E happened, an investigator will weigh the evidence in favour of E having happened against the evidence that E did not happen. The evidence will include memories, the testimony of witnesses, and our experience of what generally happens. Thus a judge or detective will weigh the evidence of one witness that Jones robbed the safe against the evidence of two witnesses that he was not in the vicinity at the time in question and evidence that Jones had never robbed a safe before. The more unusual the alleged event, the heavier is the evidence against it having happened. This is so because it is a basic principle of reasoning about matters of fact (often called by philosophers inductive reasoning) that the more often an event of a certain type A has been followed by an event of some type B, the more reason we have for expecting the next event of type A to be followed by an

13

event of type B, and the more often an event of type A has not been followed by an event of type B, the less reason we have to expect that the next one will be. Hence the more often Jones is known in certain circumstances to have robbed safes, the more reasonable it is to assume that in similar circumstances he robbed another one. The more often rods of a certain constitution have broken when subjected to a certain strain, the more reasonable it is to expect that another one will. The evidence of what usually happens counts heavily against the testimony of witnesses to what did happen. *A fortiori*, if we have evidence that on all other known occasions an event of type A has been followed by an event of type B, then the evidence is very heavy against the claim that on a particular occasion an event of type A was not followed by an event of type B. Evidence of very many such particular observations establishes those invariable correlations which we term laws of nature. Consequently all such observations count against a claim that there has been one exception to this pattern, and it would need a great deal of evidence on the other side, the testimony of many reliable witnesses, to outweigh this weight.

Thus very many astronomical and mechanical data which have been observed are instances of Newton's laws of motion. It is a consequence of Newton's laws that (given the present and past positions of Sun and planets) the Sun (relative to the Earth) never stays still. Consequently the innumerable observations which substantiate Newton's laws are counter-evidence to the claim in the Book of Joshua that for one day while the Israelites conquered the Amorites the Sun stayed still (Joshua 10:13).

'A miracle is a violation of the laws of nature; and as a firm and unalterable experience has established these laws. The proof against a miracle from the very nature of the fact, is as entire as any argument from experience can possibly be imagined. Why is it more than probable, that all men must die; that lead cannot, of itself, remain suspended in the air; that fire consumes wood, and is extinguished by water; unless it be, that these events are found agreeable to the laws of nature and there is required a violation of these laws, or in other words, a miracle to prevent them.' ([11] pp. 114 f.) Now there may be the testimony of many reliable witnesses that such an event once happened. But 'no testimony is sufficient to establish a

14

miracle, unless the testimony be of such a kind, that its false-hood would be more miraculous, than the fact, which it endeavours to establish, and even in that case there is a mutual destruction of arguments, and the superior only gives us an assurance suitable to that degree of force, which remains, after deducting the inferior' ([11] pp. 115 f.). Hence even though it be logically possible that evidence could on balance show that a law of nature had been violated, Hume claims that it is very unlikely to do so. On Hume's definition, a miracle is not merely a violation of a law of nature but one effected by a god, but Hume does not discuss what further evidence would be needed to show the violation to have been effected by a god.

Hume's subsidiary arguments

In part 2 of section x Hume goes on to produce four arguments designed to show that 'there never was a miraculous event established' in the way described. First, Hume claims that 'there is not to be found, in all history, any miracle attested by a sufficient number of men, of such unquestioned good sense, education, and learning, as to secure us against all delusion in themselves' ([11] p. 116). Secondly, he observes that men in general love to gossip about the marvellous and surprising, and that religious people do not scruple to tell falsehoods to propa-gate what they believe to be basically true. 'If the spirit of religion join itself to the love of wonder, there is an end of common sense; and human testimony, in these circumstances, loses all pretensions to authority. A religionist may be an enthusiast, and imagine he sees what has no reality: he may know his narrative to be false, and yet persevere in it, with the best intentions in the world, for the sake of promoting so holy a cause' ([11] pp. 117 f.). Thirdly, Hume claims 'it forms a strong presumption against all supernatural and miraculous relations, that they are observed chiefly to abound among ignorant and barbarous nations' ([11] p. 119).

Now these three points are purported factual claims and no one would dispute that in so far as they are correct, they tend to diminish the worth of tales of miracles. And whether they are correct is a matter for historical, rather than philosophical inquiry, and so not suitable subject matter for this book. But

15

certain general considerations are worth noting before historical inquiry is undertaken. On Hume's first point, it all depends on what counts as a 'sufficient' number of men, as 'unquestioned' good sense etc. In the passage quoted Hume suggests that his standards of evidence are high, but that it makes sense to suppose that they could be satisfied, that there could be sufficient evidence to show the occurrence of a miracle. When he comes to discuss in detail three stories of purported miracles, his standards seem to be so high that it does not make sense to suppose that there could ever be sufficient evidence to satisfy them. Consider this case:

> There surely never was a greater number of miracles ascribed to one person, than those, which were lately said to have been wrought in France upon the Tomb of Abbé Paris, the famous Jansenist, with whose sanctity the people were so long deluded. The curing of the sick, giving hearing to the deaf, and sight to the blind, were everywhere talked of as the usual effects of that holy sepulchre. But what is more extraordinary, many of the miracles were immediately proved upon the spot, before judges of unquestioned integrity, attested by witnesses of credit and distinction, in a learned age, and on the most eminent theatre that is now in the world. Nor is this all, a relation of them was published and dispersed everywhere; nor were the Jesuits, though a learned body, supported by the civil magistrate, and determined enemies to those opinions, in whose favour the miracles were said to have been wrought, ever able distinctly to refute or detect them. Where shall we find such a number of circumstances, agreeing to the corroboration of one fact? And what have we to oppose to such a cloud of witnesses, but the absolute impossibility or miraculous nature of the events, which they relate? And this surely, in the eyes of all reasonable people, will alone be regarded as a sufficient refutation ([11] p. 124 f.).

Here the credibility of the witnesses in terms of their number, integrity and education is dismissed, not as inadequate, but as irrelevant. 'The miraculous nature of the events' is alone sufficient, Hume holds, to convince 'all reasonable people' that they did not occur. What are the right standards of evidence; whether no historical evidence, or only considerable historical evidence of high quality, or less evidence would suffice to show the occurrence of a miracle is a major topic to be considered in subsequent chapters.

As regards Hume's second point, that men love to gossip about the marvellous and that religious people are none too scrupulous in their assessment of what they have observed, it must be admitted that the first sub-point *may* be true of most and the second of many people. But there are other people who are very suspicious of tales of the marvellous (and Hume himself was evidently one of them) and some religious people who lean over backwards in their attempts to report their observations honestly. How many people are in each group, and in which group are the witnesses to any alleged miracle are matters for particular historical investigation.

As regards Hume's third point, that miracles are observed chiefly to abound among ignorant and barbarous nations, it should be noted that its truth depends on what counts as an ignorant and barbarous nation. If Hume's claim is to be informative, he must not mean by an ignorant nation 'one which is disposed to believe purported miracles'. For in that case his claim would be analytically true (true, that is, in virtue of the meaning of the terms used, as is 'all bachelors are un-married'). Nor would it be a particularly interesting claim if Hume means by 'ignorant' 'not having the scientific beliefs which we have today', for clearly most nations except modern western nations would then by that definition be ignorant, and so most beliefs are likely to abound among the former nations simply because there are many more of them. But if by an 'ignorant' nation Hume means a nation lacking a literature or any sort of science, Hume's claim seems historically more dubious. Many nations, for example in the Middle Ages, with a considerable literature and a solid, although not progressive, body of scientific knowledge, have abounded with reports of miracles.

However, given these considerations, whether Hume's claims on these points are correct are matters for historical investigation rather than philosophical analysis. Hume's fourth point, designed to show that 'there never was a miraculous event established', is more in need of philosophical analysis. Hume claims that 'in matters of religion, whatever is different is contrary; and that it is impossible the religions of ancient Rome, of Turkey, of Siam, and of China should, all of them, be established on any solid foundation. Every miracle, therefore, pretended to have been wrought in any of these religions (and all of them abound in miracles), as its direct scope is to establish the particular system to which it is attributed; so has it the same force, though more indirectly, to overthrow every other system. In destroying a rival system, it likewise destroys the credit of those miracles, on which that system was established' ([11] pp. 121 f.). The argument is that if a miracle of ancient Graeco-Roman religion occurred as described, that is evidence that the gods of the Greeks and Romans exist, and if a Christian miracle occurred as described, that is evidence that the God of Christians exists. But if the gods of the Greeks and Romans exist, the God of the Christians does not, and conversely. Therefore the evidence in favour of a Graeco-Roman miracle is evidence against the existence of the God of the Christians, and hence evidence against the occurrence of Christian miracles, and conversely. Now there is no doubt about the fact that adherents of many different systems of religion report events as miracles wrought by their god or gods. What is of interest is whether the evidence they adduce shows the miracle to have been performed by one of their gods, and whether the existence of their god or gods is or is not compatible with the existence of a different god. These philosophical questions will receive attention in Chapter 5.

Recent writers in the Humean Tradition

The general argument which Hume gives in part 1 against the occurrence of miracles has been taken up and developed by number of recent writers in the British empirical tradition. We saw that Hume's official view there was that it is logically possible that the balance of evidence could show that a law of nature had been violated and so support the occurrence of a miracle, but very very strong evidence of testimony etc. would be needed for this to happen. But we also noticed in Hume's detailed discussion of purported miracles a stronger position, that no amount of evidence that an event E happened on a particular occasion could ever be stronger than the evidence supporting a law of nature, a consequence of which was that E

18

could not and so did not happen. Among recent writers Professor Antony Flew has defended this stronger position. In his book *Hume's Philosophy of Belief*, in his discussion of the section on miracles he writes as follows:

> The justification for giving the 'scientific' this ultimate precedence here over the 'historical' lies in the nature of the propositions concerned and in the evidence which can be displayed to sustain them . . . the candidate historical proposition will be particular, often singular, and in the past tense. . . . But just by reason of this very pastness and particularity it is no longer possible for anyone to examine the subject directly for himself . . . the law of nature will, unlike the candidate historical proposition, be a general nomological. It can thus in theory, though obviously not always in practice, be tested at any time by any person ([16] p. 207 f.).

In recent philosophical writing on the topic two points have been made additional to Hume's to support his contention or the stronger contention of Flew. The first is that evidence that a particular event E occurred and that it is a violation of a supposed law of nature L really only tends to show, not that a law of nature has been violated, but that we have misstated the laws of nature. The real law of nature is not really L but some other law L^1 which allows the occurrence of E. Thus it might be supposed that it is contrary to the well established laws of gravity, hydrodynamics etc. for a man to walk on water. Now suppose witnesses report that Jones walked on water. The evidence supporting the currently accepted laws of gravity, hydrostatics etc. is against them. But if the witnesses are in fact correct in affirming that Jones walked on water, all that shows is that the laws of gravity and hydrostatics are not as simple as we had supposed at first. The laws postulated must be adjusted so as to allow that under certain circumstances (e.g. when the man is a man of great faith) men can walk on water. This view amounts to the view that it is logically impossible that there be a violation of a law of nature. One or two recent articles incorporate this view. Thus, for example, Alastair McKinnon writes:

> The idea of a suspension of natural law is self-contradictory. . . . This contradiction may stand out more clearly if for

19

natural law we substitute the expression *the actual course of events*. *Miracle* would then be defined as 'an event involving the suspension of the actual course of events'. And someone who insisted on describing an event as a miracle would be in the rather odd position of claiming that its occurrence was contrary to the actual course of events ([20] p. 309).

The laws of nature state what happens. Consequently everything that happens must accord with them.

A second point is that even if one could show that an event had occurred which was a violation of a law of nature, that would not show that a miracle had occurred. A violation of a law of nature is only a miracle if caused by a god. But if an event has a cause, then in citing the cause we explain its occurrence. But, the objection goes, explaining anything consists in showing that its occurrence was in accordance with some law of nature. So whatever can be explained is no violation of a law. Nowell-Smith argues against an opponent on these lines:

Let him consider the meaning of the word 'explanation' and let him ask himself whether this notion does not involve that of a law or hypothesis capable of predictive expansion. And then let him ask himself whether such an explanation would not be natural, in whatever terms it was couched, and how the notion of 'the supernatural' could play any part in it ([15] p. 253).

Many other modern philosophers have written articles and chapters of books in this Humean tradition of writing on miracles. The Humean tradition is the tradition that there is a very high improbability (if not a logical impossibility) in the balance of evidence favouring the occurrence of a miracle in the sense of a violation of a law of nature by a god; this improbability arising not from empirical considerations, such as current lack of relevant historical evidence or difficulty of acquiring it, but from logical considerations, in virtue of what we mean by 'violation', 'evidence', 'law of nature' etc. Many modern writers have, as we have seen, gone beyond Hume in claiming not merely that it is highly improbable, but that it is logically impossible that the balance of evidence should favour the occurrence of a miracle; that is, that it does not make sense to suppose that the balance of evidence should be thus.

To assess the worth of such claims we must analyse carefully what would constitute: (i) a violation of a law of nature; (ii) evidence that a particular historical event had occurred; (iii) evidence that such an event was due to the action of a god. With the aid of various modern philosophical results and techniques, we shall investigate these questions in the next four chapters, and then will be in a better position to assess the worth of the claims of the Humean tradition. I shall assume throughout Chapters 3, 4 and 5 that we have no evidence for or against the existence of a god other than historical and scientific evidence for or against the occurrence of miracles. In Chapter 6 I will abandon this artificial restriction.

3 Violation of a Law of Nature

Laws of nature

The task of the theoretical scientist is to set forth the laws of nature (which may be physical, chemical, biological or psychological laws, or laws of any other science). In any field he will have a number of observational results. He seeks the most natural generalisation or extrapolation of those results, or, as I shall put it, the simplest formula from which the past results can be deduced.

In a primitive way ordinary people generalise their observations in the most natural or simple way to obtain general statements about how things behave, from which they can deduce how things will behave in future. Thus, to take a well-worn example, suppose that swans had not previously been observed and then we observe in different parts of England a number of swans and find them all to be white. We might set forward a hypothesis 'all swans are white'. This allows us to infer of each past swan observed that it was white, and predicts of each future swan which will be observed that it will be white. Another formula equally compatible with observations to date, but making different predictions is 'all swans in England are white, but elsewhere are black'. Yet this would never be seriously proposed because it is so obviously less simple than, a less natural extrapolation from the data than, the alternative formula.

The task of the scientist may thus be compared to that of a man finding a formula governing the occurrence of points on a graph. Compatible with any finite set of data, there will always be an infinite number of possible formulae from which the data can be predicted. We can rule out many by further tests, but however many tests we make we shall still have only a finite number of data and hence an infinite number of formulae compatible with them. Yet some of these formulae will be highly complex relative to the data so that no scientist would consider that the data provided evidence that those formulae were laws of nature. Others are very simple formulae such that the data can be said to provide evidence that they are laws of nature. Thus suppose the scientist finds marks at $(1,1)$, $(2,2)$, $(3,3)$, and $(4,4)$, the first number of each pair being the x-coordinate and the second the y-coordinate. One formula which would predict these marks is $x = y$. Another one is $(x-1)(x-2)(x-3)(x-4) + x = y$. But clearly we would not regard the data as supporting the second formula. It is too clumsy a formula to explain four observations. Among simple formulae supported by the data, the simplest is the best supported and regarded, provisionally, as correct. If the formula survives further tests, that increases the evidence in its favour as a law.

What counts as a formula of sufficient simplicity to be adopted as a law and so used for prediction in the absence of simpler formulae is a matter of the quantity and variety of the data on the basis of which it is constructed. While

$$(x-1)(x-2)(x-3)(x-4) + x = y$$

would not do if supported only by the four cited data, it could reasonably be put forward on the basis of four hundred data. Einstein's field equations of General Relativity could hardly be put forward solely on the basis of observations of the movement of Mercury's perihelion (observations compatible with those equations) but could be put forward on the basis of an enormous number of terrestrial and planetary motions and of optical phenomena, previously accounted for by Newtonian mechanics or the Special Theory of Relativity, and of certain further phenomena (such as the movement of Mercury's perihelion) not compatible with the latter theories.

Often, unlike in my two initial examples, a number or different formulae of similar simplicity (no one clearly simpler than the rest) are equally compatible with past data, yet, being different formulae, make different predictions for the future. An artificial example of this would be if we had a number of points on a graph which could be fitted on to hyperbolic curves of different eccentricity but not on to any simpler curves (e.g. a straight line). More complicated real-life examples are provided by current cosmological theories, e.g. 'big bang' and 'steady state' theories. They all take account of the same data of astronomy and mechanics, yet integrate these in different ways so as to get different predictions. Yet many of them seem equally

24

simple, no one a more natural extrapolation from the data than the others. In such cases, in so far as he can, a scientist will test between conflicting predictions and reject those formulae which yield incorrect predictions. If he can do this and is left with only one formula compatible with the data of observation, then he will adopt that.

Sometimes the scientist will be able to see no simple formula, that is formula of sufficient simplicity, compatible with a collection of data in some field, and in that case will not feel justified in adopting any one formula and making predictions on the basis of it. If in our studies of swans we had observed in England several white, several black, and several red ones with no obvious pattern of geographical distribution, we would not be able to produce any simple formula covering these data which would enable us to predict the colours of future swans. In so far as a formula is simple and the simplest known formula compatible with observations, we regard it – provisionally – as a law of nature. Any proposed law of nature will be corrigible – that is, future observations could show the proposed law not to be a true law. But in so far as a formula survives further tests, that increases the evidence in its favour as a true law.

Another example of these points is provided by Kepler's work on planetary motion. Studying the positions of planets observed during the previous thirty years, Kepler sought formulae from which those results could be deduced. But not any formulae would do; the formulae would have to be formulae of fairly simple curves, describing each planet as having travelled along a curve of that type, in order for us to be justified in supposing that the formulae described the future as well as the past behaviour of planets. If the formulae were simply records of past positions with unrelated predictions attached, we would not, despite the fact that they accurately recorded past positions, think ourselves justified in believing the future predictions yielded by them. Only if they were the formulae of simple curves which fitted the past positions would we think that we could predict from them. Kepler eventually fitted the positions of each planet on to an ellipse, having the Sun at one focus. The neat fit of the past positions on to this curve justified men in supposing that planets in future would travel in elliptical paths.

The general points of the last few pages would, I believe – with qualifications and additions – be accepted by most philosophers of science. Philosophers of science today are very concerned to bring out clearly and explicitly the criteria for choosing between alternative theories equally compatible with observations obtained so far, criteria which, in common with many philosophers of science, I have termed criteria of simplicity. But although philosophers may still disagree about exactly what those criteria are, they agree that such criteria operate, and they agree in many particular cases when two different theories equally compatible with observations obtained to date are constructed which of the two is to be preferred.

The upshot of all this is that – against McKinnon – (see pp. 19 f.) laws of nature do not just describe what happens ('the actual course of events'). They describe what happens in a regular and predictable way. When what happens is entirely irregular and unpredictable, its occurrence is not something describable by natural laws.

Meaning of 'Violation of a law of nature'

Given this understanding of a law of nature, what is meant by a violation of a law of nature? I think that those who, like Hume, have used this or a similar expression have intended to mean by it an occurence of a non-repeatable counter-instance to a law of nature (this useful definition is provided by Professor Ninian Smart in his discussion of Hume's account of miracles [17]). The use of the definiens and of the definiendum, violation of a law of nature, both assume that the operation of a law of nature is logically compatible with the occurrence of an exception to its operation. This point will be developed below.

Clearly, as we have noted, events contrary to predictions of formulae which we had good reason to believe to be laws of nature often occur. But if we have good reason to believe that they have occurred and good reason to believe that similar events would occur in similar circumstances, then undoubtedly we have good reason to believe that the formulae which we previously believed to be the laws of nature were not in fact such laws. For then the real laws of nature will, we can best suppose, be the old purported laws with a modification for the circumstances in question. There cannot be repeatable counter-instances to genuine laws of nature, that is, counter-instances

26

which would be repeated in similar circumstances. Repeatable counter-instances to purported laws only show those purported laws not to be genuine laws.

But what are we to say if we have good reason to believe that an event E has occurred contrary to predictions of a formula L which otherwise we have good reason to believe to be a law of nature, and we have good reason to believe that events similar to E would not occur in circumstances as similar as we like in any respect to those of the occurrence of E? E would then be a non-repeatable counter-instance to L. In this case we could say *either* (as before) that L cannot be the law of nature operative in the field, since an exception to its operation has occurred, *or* that L is the law of nature operative in the field, but that an exceptional non-repeatable counter-instance to its occurrence has occurred. The advantage of saying the former is particularly obvious where universal laws are involved. As a universal law has the form 'so-and-sos always do such and such', it seems formally incompatible with a counter-instance reported by 'this is a so-and-so, and did not do such-and-such'. Both statements cannot be true together, the argument goes; evidence in favour of the exception is evidence against the purported law. The advantage of saying the latter is however this. The evidence shows that we cannot replace L by a more successful law allowing us to predict E as well as other phenomena supporting L. For any modified formula which allowed us to predict E would allow us to predict similar events in similar circumstances and hence, *ex hypothesi*, we have good reason to believe, would give false predictions. Whereas if we leave the formula L unmodified, it will, we have good reason to believe, give correct predictions in all other conceivable circumstances. Hence if we are to say that any law of nature is operative in the field in question we must say that it is L. The only alternative is to say that no law of nature operates in the field. Yet saying this does not seem to do justice to the (in general) enormous success of L in predicting occurrences in the field.

For these latter reasons it seems not unnatural to describe E as a non-repeatable counter-instance to a law of nature L. If we do say this we have to understand the operation of a universal law of the form 'so-and-so's always do such-and-such' as logically compatible with 'this is a so-and-so and does not do such-and-such'. To say that a certain such formula is a law is to say that

27

in general its predictions are true and that any exceptions to its operation cannot be accounted for by another formula which could be taken as a law (by the criteria discussed earlier). One must thus distinguish between a formula being a law *and* a formula being (universally) true or being a law which holds without exception.

I believe this second account of the way to describe the relation between a formula which otherwise we have good reason to believe to be a law of nature, and an isolated exception to it, to be more natural than the first, that is, to do more justice to the way in which most of us ordinarily talk about these matters. However that may be, it is clearly a coherent way of talking, and it is the way adopted by those who talk of violations of natural laws. For if any exception to its operation was incompatible with a law being a true law, there appears to be no ready sense which could be given to 'a violation of a law of nature'. Hence I shall in future presuppose the second account. Since the second account is a possible account, the concept of a violation of a law of nature is coherent, and we must reject the views of McKinnon and others who claim that it is not logically possible that a law of nature be violated.

If, as seems natural, we understand by the physically impossible what is ruled out by a law of nature, then our account of laws of nature suggests that it makes sense to suppose that on occasion the physically impossible occurs. (If this seems too paradoxical a thing to say we shall have to give a different sense to the 'physically impossible'.) Substantially the same conclusion is reached by Holland [18]. For Holland a violation of a law of nature is a 'conceptual impossibility'. He terms it this because the supposition that there is an object behaving in a way other than that laid down by laws of nature is the supposition that there is an object behaving in ways other than the ways embodied in our normal understanding of it, and so, in wide senses of 'involved' and 'concept', involved in our ordinary concept of it. Therefore, having shown that it makes sense to suppose a law of nature violated, Holland argues that in such a case the conceptually impossible would occur. That being so, he concludes, one cannot deduce from a thing having happened that it is a possible occurrence – *ab esse ad posse non valet consequentia*. (When assessing Holland's conclusion, we should remember what he means by 'conceptual

28

impossibility'. He does not mean what most philosophers mean by that expression – viz. something the description of which involves a self-contradiction – but merely something the occurrence of which is ruled out by our ordinary (and with this exception basically correct) understanding of the way objects behave.)

Evidence as to which events, if they occurred, would be violations of laws of nature

The crucial question however is what would be good reason for believing that an event E, if it occurred, was a non-repeatable as opposed to a repeatable counter-instance to a formula L which we have on all other evidence good reason to believe to be a law of nature. The evidence that E is a repeatable counter-instance would be that a new formula L^1 better confirmed than L as a law of nature can be set up, which, unlike L, predicted E. A formula is confirmed by data, it will be recalled, in so far as the data obtained so far are predicted by the formula, new predictions are successful, and the formula is a simple one relative to the collection of data (viz. a natural extrapolation from the data). Now L^1 will be better confirmed than L if it, like L, predicts the data so far obtained, other than E; unlike L, predicts E; and is no more complex than L. If it is considerably more complex than L, that counts against it and might perhaps balance the fact that it, unlike L, predicts E. And if it is so much more complicated than L that it is not of sufficient simplicity relative to the data (see our earlier discussion) to be a law of nature, it will clearly have to be rejected. In so far as there is a doubt whether any proposed law L^1 is more satisfactory than L, clearly the scientist will, if he can, test between the further predictions of the two laws. If, for matters where they make conflicting predictions, L^1 predicts successfully and L unsuccessfully, L^1 will be preferred, and vice versa. It follows from all this that L will have to be retained as a law of nature and E regarded as a non-repeatable counter-instance to it, if any proposed rival formula L^1 were too much more complicated than L without giving better new predictions, or predicted new phenomena unsuccessfully where L predicted successfully. L^1 would certainly be too much more complicated if it were not

29

of sufficient simplicity relative to the data to be a law of nature at all (see our earlier discussion). L would have to be abandoned if some proposed rival formula L^1 which predicted E were not much more complicated than L, or predicted new phenomena successfully where L predicted unsuccessfully.

Here is an example. Suppose E to be the levitation (i.e. rising into the air and remaining floating on it, in circumstances where no known forces other than gravity (e.g. magnetism) are acting) of a certain holy person. E is thus a counter-instance to otherwise well-substituted laws of nature L (viz. the laws of mechanics, electro-magnetism etc.) which together purport to give an account of all the forces operating in nature. We could show E to be a repeatable counter-instance if we could construct a formula L^1 which predicted E and also successfully predicted other divergencies from L, as well as all other tested predictions of L; *or* if we could construct L^1 which was comparatively simple relative to the data and predicted E and all the other tested predictions of L, but predicted divergencies from L which had not yet been tested. L^1 might differ from L in postulating the operation of an entirely new kind of force, e.g. that under certain curcumstances bodies exercise a gravitational repulsion on each other, and those circumstances would include the circumstances in which E occurred. If L^1 satisfied either of the above two conditions, we would adopt it, and we would then say that under certain circumstances people do levitate and so E was not a counter-instance to a law of nature. However it might be that any modification which we made to the laws of nature to allow them to predict E might not yield any more successful predictions than L and they might be so clumsy that there was no reason to believe that their predictions not yet tested would be successful. Under these circumstances we would have good reason to believe that the levitation of the holy person violated the laws of nature.

If the laws of nature are statistical and not universal, as – see p. 3 – Quantum Theory suggests, it is not in all cases so clear what counts as a counter-instance to them. A universal law is a law of the form 'all so-and-sos do such-and-such', and a counter-instance is therefore a so-and-so which does not do such-and-such. The occurrence of such a counter-instance is the occurrence of an exception to the law. A statistical law is a law of the form 'n% of so-and-sos do such-and-such'. But here however many

30

so-and-sos are observed which do not do such-and-such, their occurrence is not completely ruled out by the theory. The theory tells us the proportion of so-and-sos which do such-and-such in an infinite class, and however many so-and-sos are found not to do such-and-such in a finite class, this finite class may be just an unrepresentative selection from the infinite class. It *may* be. But if something occurs which, given the truth of the law, is highly unlikely, that counts against the law, is counter-evidence to it, even if not formally ruled out by it. If the proportion of so-and-sos which do such-and-such in one of the very few, albeit large, finite classes studied is vastly different from that stated to hold in the law, that is counter-evidence to the law. Such an event is therefore not unnaturally described as an exception to a statistical law and the question can therefore be discussed whether it is a repeatable or a non-repeatable exception. It is formally compatible with the currently accepted statistical version of the second law of thermodynamics that a kettle of water put on a fire freeze instead of boiling. But it is vastly improbable that such an event will ever happen within human experience. Hence if it does happen, it is not unnaturally described as an exception to the law. If the evidence does not lead to our adopting a rival law, the event can then be described as a violation of the second law of thermodynamics. Any who speak of a violation of statistical laws would presumably mean the occurrence of a non-repeatable counter-instance to such laws, in the above sense of counter-instance.

All claims about what are the laws of nature are corrigible. However much support any purported law has at the moment, one day it may prove to be no true law. So likewise will be all claims about what does or does not violate the laws of nature. When an event apparently violates such laws, the appearance may arise simply because no one has thought of the true law which could explain the event, or, while they have thought of it, it is so complex relative to the data as rightly to be dismissed before even being tested, or too complex to be adopted without further testing and the tests too difficult in practice to carry out. New scientific knowledge may later turn up which forces us to revise any such claims about what violates laws of nature. But then all claims to knowledge about the physical world are corrigible, and we must reach provisional conclusions about them on the evidence available to us. We have to some extent

31

good evidence about what are the laws of nature, and some of them are so well established and account for so many data that any modifications to them which we could suggest to account for the odd counter-instance would be so clumsy and *ad hoc* as to upset the whole structure of science. In such cases the evidence is strong that if the purported counter-instance occurred it was a violation of the law of nature. There is good reason to believe that the following events, if they occurred, would be violations of the laws of nature: levitation; resurrection from the dead in full health of a man whose heart has not been beating for twenty-four hours and who was dead also by other currently used criteria; water turning into wine without the assistance of chemical apparatus or catalysts; a man getting better from polio in a minute. We know quite enough about how things behave to be reasonably certain that, in the sense earlier (p. 28) delineated, these events are physically impossible.

4 Historical Evidence

The claim of the last chapter was that we could have good reason to suppose that an event E, if it occurred, was a violation of a law of nature L. But could one have good evidence that such an event E occurred? At this point we must face the force of Hume's own argument. This, it will be remembered, runs as follows. The evidence, which *ex hypothesi* is good evidence, that L is a law of nature is evidence that E did not occur. We have certain other evidence that E did occur. In such circumstances, writes Hume, the wise man 'weighs the opposite experiments. He considers which side is supported by the greater number of experiments' ([11] p. 111). Since he supposes that the evidence that E occurred would be that of testimony, Hume concludes 'that no testimony is sufficient to establish a miracle, unless the testimony be of such a kind, that its falsehood would be more miraculous, than the fact which it endeavours to establish' ([11] pp. 115 f.). Flew, it will be remembered, went further and claimed that because of the 'nature of the propositions concerned' ([16] p. 208) the evidence never could be that strong. In order to assess the worth of this claim we must digress and see in general how historical evidence is weighed.

Four kinds of historical evidence

We have four kinds of evidence about what happened at some past instant— our own apparent memories of our past experiences, the testimony of others about their past experiences, physical traces and our contemporary understanding of what things are physically impossible or improbable. (The fourth is only a corrective to the other three, not an independent source of detailed information.) A piece of evidence gives grounds for believing that some past event occurred, except in so far as it conflicts with other pieces of evidence. In so far as pieces of

33

evidence conflict, they have to be weighed against each other.

Let us consider more fully the kinds of evidence. Firstly we have our own apparent memories. I remember, in my opinion, to some extent what I was doing yesterday or last year, what happened to me, and what was going on in the neighbourhood. True, though I may think that I remember these things I may be mistaken, and evidence of other types about what happened may convince me that I am mistaken. However in the usual use of 'remember', if I remember that p, then of logical necessity it was the case that p. Hence the memory evidence for what happened to be weighed against other evidence is best described as evidence of apparent memory. While I may be mistaken about what happened (my claims to memory may be wrong), I can be certain about my apparent memories. Secondly we have the testimony of others – what they say that they did and saw and what happened to them. This may be testimony spoken to us personally or written down long ago. Thirdly we have physical traces of what happened – footprints, fingerprints, ashes, bomb craters. Such physical states are evidence for us that certain past events probably happened, of which events they may be termed traces. A particular present state or event, that is change of state, A_1 is a trace for us of a particular past state or event B_1 if the two events are members of classes of events A's and B's, when the occurrence of A's is highly correlated in our experience with prior occurrence of B's. (1) This correlation (unless – which is highly unlikely – it is coincidental) will arise either because B's cause A's (and A's are seldom caused by anything else) or because C's cause both B's and A's, first B's and then later A's (and A's are seldom caused by anything else). Thus a particular human footprint (in the sense of a mark in the shape of a human foot) in the sand is for us a trace that someone with a foot of that size has walked there recently, because we have observed that men walking on sand produce footprints, and that these are seldom produced by any other cause. Fourthly we have our contemporary understanding of what things are physically impossible or improbable, that is, ruled out or rendered improbable by the laws of nature or generalisations of what usually happens. This scientific knowledge serves as a check on the evidence of apparent memory, testimony and traces. Evidence as to what is physically impossible is, as Hume emphasised, a very strong

34

check on other evidence. If a witness says that he saw a man recover within a minute from polio, or a man walk on air, we, with our contemporary scientific knowledge, have reason to believe that such things are not physically possible, and so have strong evidence against that testimony. Evidence about what is physically improbable is a check, but a less strong one, on other evidence. It counts against evidence that Smith was dealt all thirteen cards of a suit one Friday night at bridge that only extremely rarely are all thirteen cards of a suit dealt at bridge to one player's hand, i.e. that such an event is highly improbable.

My classification of kinds of evidence is, I believe, exhaustive (viz. there are no other kinds), but the classes do to some extent overlap. Thus testimony to the occurrence of X may also be a trace of an event Y. If Jones tells the police that Smith did the robbery, then this event is testimony to Smith having done the robbery. But if we know that on past occasions Jones has only betrayed men to the police when Mrs Jones has persuaded him to do so, then on this occasion his telling the police is also a trace of Mrs Jones having persuaded him to do so.

Now it will be evident from the account which I gave in Chapter 2 of Hume's discussion of miracles that Hume says a great deal about evidence of the second and fourth kinds, but nothing at all about evidence of the first and third kinds. Hume supposes that the conflict about what happens is a conflict between testimony and scientific knowledge. And so no doubt were most conflicts known to Hume – e.g. conflicts about whether the biblical miracles took place. But sometimes the evidence available to an inquirer consists not merely of the testimony of others but of one's own apparently remembered observations. Some men have the evidence of their own eyes, not merely the testimony of others. What, one wonders, would Hume say, if he himself apparently saw a man walk on water? And Hume says nothing at all about traces, fingerprints, footprints and cigarette ash, the impersonal kind of evidence on which detectives like to rely a great deal. But then Hume lived before the era of scientific criminology, and so would hardly be likely to be aware of what could be established by such methods.

However, the evidence of traces' could be of considerable importance in assessing whether some event E occurred which if it occurred would have violated a law of nature. Thus if E

35

consists in a state X being followed by a state Y, and we have a trace of the state X and an observed later state Y, or a trace thereof, then we have evidence of traces that E occurred. Thus we might have evidence of footprints in soft mud that Jones was on one side of a broad river one minute ago, and evidence of Jones on the other side now not in the least wet, with not the slightest indication of water having touched his body or clothes (viz. no traces of his having swum across the river), and no bridge, boats, aeroplanes or rope by which he could have crossed. Hence the evidence indicates that he must have walked or flown across. Traces alone, unsupported by testimony, could thus provide evidence that such an event occurred.

It must, however, be admitted that traces are of more use in inquiring into alleged recent miracles than into alleged miracles of long ago. For it is a sad fact which detectives bemoan that many traces become obliterated in the course of time. Foorprints in the sand and cigarette ash still warm are useful indications of what happened a minute or two ago – but footprints get smudged out, and ash gets cold and scattered, and they do not serve as indications of what happened centuries ago. Yet there are many traces which do not become obliterated and which historians are now learning to use – C_{14} dating to determine the age of artefacts, errors of transcription to determine the history of documents, peculiarities of style to determine authorship etc. Science is continually discovering new kinds of traces which reveal facets of ancient history. Who knows how much detail about the past the science of the future will be able to infer from then current remains?

So much for the kinds of evidence which we have about the past and their sources. Clearly one piece of evidence will often conflict with another. The testimony of Jones may conflict with what I appear to remember, or with the testimony of Smith. Jones says that he stayed with Robinson at home all day yesterday, while I 'distinctly remember' having seen him at the Pig and Whistle, and Smith claims to have seen him at the Horse and Hounds. Testimony may conflict with traces. Jones has a scar of a certain type normally caused by a knife wound, but denies having been slashed. Or traces may conflict with each other. A bomb crater may indicate a recent explosion, but the healthy state of the surrounding vegetation count against this. And our contemporary understanding of the physically

36

possible may count against the evidence of particular traces, testimony or apparent memory. I appear to remember having seen the conjurer take the rabbit out of the hat, but he cannot have done so, because the laws of light are such that, had the rabbit been in the hat, I would have seen it.

Principles for weighing conflicting evidence

Conflicting evidence has to be weighed, and the fundamental idea involved in such weighing seems to be to obtain as coherent a picture as possible of the past as consistent as possible with the evidence. We can express this idea in the form of one basic principle for assessing evidence and several subsidiary principles limiting its operation. The most basic principle is to accept as many pieces of evidence as possible. If one witness says one thing, and five witnesses say a different thing, then, in the absence of further evidence (e.g. about their unreliability) take the testimony of the latter. If one method of dating an artefact gives one result, and five methods give a different result, then, in the absence of further information accept the latter result.

The first subsidiary principle is – apart from any empirical evidence about their relative reliability – that evidence of different kinds ought to be given different weights. How this is to be done can only be illustrated by examples. Thus one's own apparent memory ought as such to count for more than the testimony of another witness (unless and until evidence of its relative unreliability is forthcoming). If I appear to remember having seen Jones yesterday in Hull, but Brown says that he had Jones under observation all day yesterday and that he went nowhere near to Hull, then – *ceteris paribus* – I ought to stand by my apparent memory. This is because when someone else gives testimony it always makes sense to suppose that he is lying; whereas, when I report to myself what I appear to remember, I cannot be lying. For the liar is someone who says what he believes to be false. But if I report what I appear to remember (and I can *know* for certain what I appear to remember), I cannot be lying. Secondly, if I feel highly confident that I remember some event, my apparent memory ought to count for more than if I am only moderately confident. My apparent memory has a built-in weight, apart from empirical

37

evidence which may be forthcoming about its reliability in different circumstances (e.g. that it is not reliable when I am drunk). In these and other ways for non-empirical reasons different pieces of evidence ought to be given different weights in assessing the balance of evidence.

The second subsidiary principle is that different pieces of evidence ought to be given different weights in accordance with any empirical evidence which may be available about their different reliability, obtained by a procedure which I may term narrowing the evidence class. In general we necessarily assume or have reason to believe that apparent memory, testimony and states of particular types are reliable evidence about past states and events. But clash of evidence casts doubt on this. So we test the reliability of a piece of evidence by classifying it as a member of a narrow class, and investigating the reliability of other members of that class which – see note 1 to page 34 – would have to be classes whose members were described by projectible predicates. If the testimony of Jones conflicts with the testimony of Smith, then we must investigate not the worth of testimony in general, but the worth of Jones' testimony and of Smith's testimony. We do this by seeing if on all other occasions when we can ascertain what happened Jones or Smith correctly described what happened. In so far as each did, his testimony is reliable. Now this procedure will only work in so far as we can at some stage ascertain with sufficient certainty what happened without bringing in empirical evidence about the reliability of the evidence about what happened. Unless we could establish with sufficient certainty by mere balance of evidence what happened on a certain past occasion, without testing the worth of each piece of evidence by considering the worth of evidence of a narrow class to which it belongs, we could never establish anything at all. For the testing of evidence of one class can only be performed if we presuppose the reliability in general of other evidence. Thus, to test Jones' testimony we have to find out – by the testimony of others and traces – what happened on a number of occasions and then see whether Jones correctly reported this. But to do this we have to be able to ascertain what did happen on those occasions, and we will have various pieces of evidence as well as that of Jones about this. Unless the agreement of evidence apart from the testimony of Jones suffices to do this, we could never show Jones to be a reliable

38

or unreliable witness. We may have empirical evidence about the reliability of such other evidence, but as such evidence will consist of more empirical evidence, we have to stop somewhere, with evidence which we can take to be reliable without empirical evidence thereof.

Similar tests to these tests of the reliability of testimony can be made of the reliability of traces, e.g. of methods of dating ancient documents.

For a given number of pieces of evidence in the class, the narrower the evidence class chosen for the assessment of the worth of a particular piece of evidence, the more reliable the assessment yielded by it. If we examine the worth of a particular piece of testimony given by a certain Soviet diplomat, Stamkovsky, to an official of M.I.5 by examining the worth of n pieces of testimony given by Soviet diplomats, then we have some knowledge of its worth, better than our knowledge of the worth of testimony in general. But we have a better assessment of its worth if we examine the worth of n pieces of testimony given by Stamkovsky and an even better estimate if we consider the worth of n pieces of testimony given by Stamkovsky to British counter-intelligence officers. But this raises a well-known difficulty about evidence classes – that the narrower the evidence class we choose, the fewer pieces of evidence we will have on which to base our assessment. We will have plenty of pieces of evidence by Soviet diplomats the reliability of which we can check, but few pieces of evidence given by Stamkovsky to British counter-intelligence agents the reliability of which we can check. The narrower the evidence class the better, but so long only as we have sufficient evidence to put in it to reach a well-substantiated conclusion.

The third subsidiary principle is not to reject coincident evidence (unless the evidence of its falsity is extremely strong) unless an explanation can be given of the coincidence; and the better substantiated is that explanation, the more justified the rejection of the coincident evidence. If five witnesses all say the same thing and we wish to reject their evidence, we are in general not justified in doing so unless we can explain why they all said the same thing. Such explanations could be that they were subject to common illusions, or all plotted together to give false testimony. The better substantiated is such an explanation the better justified is our rejection of the evidence. Substantiation of the theory of a common plot would be provided by evidence that the witnesses were all seen together before the event, that they stood to gain from giving false testimony etc. But ultimately the evidence rests on evidence about particular past events and would itself need to be substantiated in ways earlier described.

These subsidiary principles, and perhaps others which I have not described, then qualify the basic principle of accepting the majority of the evidence. They are the standards of investigation adopted, I would claim, by and large by all historical investigators.

However, those whose standards of historical evidence are by and large very similar may have *slightly* different standards, and with their slightly different standards may reach different conclusions about which way the balance of evidence tends. Such disputes will arise between people who in general accept the principles of evidence which I set forward, but who differ about the details or the interpretation of these principles, or the different weight to be given to each principle.

I stated the principles in a fairly general way which all would accept, but when we come down to details and interpretation differences are likely to arise. Thus I described the basic principle as that of accepting as many pieces of evidence as possible. But what constitutes one piece of evidence? Does each footprint constitute separate evidence of a man's presence, or is a set of footprints just one piece of evidence? Are fingerprints separate evidence from footprints? The subsidiary principles are also open to an enormous variety of interpretations – if I am absolutely convinced that I remember some event, how many pieces of confidently given testimony ought to make me abandon my claim? And how ought one to narrow the evidence class? Given that the class of all pieces of testimony made by Soviet diplomats the truth or falsity of which we can ascertain independently is too wide a class for ascertaining the value of Stamkovsky's testimony to an M.I.5 official, how shall we narrow it? Shall we choose the class of all pieces of testimony given to British counter-intelligence agents by Soviet diplomats the truth or falsity of which we can ascertain independently? Or the class of all pieces of testimony given by Stamkovsky to anyone the truth of falsity of which we can ascertain independently? And so on.

In answer to these questions a number of standard examples can sometimes be provided which illustrate the correct application of the basic or subsidiary principles. We can give examples in detail of witnesses whose combined testimony ought to outweigh a firm claim to memory, of good and bad explanations of the occurrence of coincident but false evidence. Or further principles, which I shall term minor principles, can sometimes be provided which show how different kinds of evidence ought to be taken into account. Thus if in general we can show that the behaviour of individuals in different circumstances is more of a pattern than is the behaviour of members of a group in similar circumstances, that would show that the reliability of Stamkovsky's testimony to an M.I.5 official is better estimated by the reliability of Stamkovsky's testimony to anyone than by the reliability of the testimony of Soviet diplomats to British counter-intelligence agents. But how we apply this principle depends on what counts as 'a group' and 'similar circumstances'. Further principles and examples could perhaps elucidate this. But there will be people who will dispute more generally accepted standards in some of these matters, disagreeing with our standard examples or minor principles. With regard to some minor principles or standard examples people may indeed be evenly divided – there may be no generally accepted standards. In such a case when the area of disagreement is fairly small argument can take place. Argument will consist in a man trying to show his opponent that the opponent's disputed principle coheres less well with commonly accepted principles of evidence than does a rival principle of his own; or that a standard example proffered by the opponent is importantly unlike the other standard examples on which both would agree. These points about the nature of argument in such cases will be confirmed by considering how people do and can argue about the principles in dispute crucial for our topic of miracles.

Principles for assessing conflicts between evidence of the first three kinds and evidence of the fourth kind

Bearing in mind these considerations about conflicting evidence and these principles for assessing different ways of weighing evidence, what about a conflict between evidence of the first three kinds that an event E occurred and evidence of the fourth kind that an event of the type of E is physically impossible? Hume's official answer, it will be remembered, was that exceedingly strong evidence of other kinds, in particular testimony, would be needed for evidence about physical impossibility to be outweighed. Flew's more extreme answer, an answer also suggested by Hume's detailed discussion of three purported miracles, is that the latter evidence could never be outweighed. It will be remembered (see p. 19) that Flew gave as justification for his claim that while a historical proposition concerned a past event of which we have only the present remains (viz. evidence of the first three kinds), the scientific proposition, being a general statement (viz. about all entities of some kind at all times and places), can go on and on being tested by any person who wishes to test it. Flew's suggestion seems to be that the historical proposition cannot go on and on being tested by any person at any time.

If this is Flew's contrast, it is mistaken. Particular experiments on particular occasions only give a certain and far from conclusive support to claims that a purported scientific law is true. Any person can test for the truth of a purported scientific law, but a positive result to one test will give only limited support to the claim. Exactly the same holds for purported historical truths. Anyone can examine the evidence, but a particular piece of evidence gives only limited support to the claim that the historical proposition is true. But in the historical as in the scientific case, there is no limit to the testing which we can do. We can go on and on testing for the truth of historical as of scientific propositions. True, the actual traces, apparent memories and testimony, which I may term the direct evidence, available to an inquirer are unlikely to increase in number, at any rate after a certain time. Only so many witnesses will have seen the event in question and once their testimony has been obtained no more will be available. Further, it is an unfortunate physical fact, as we have noted, that many traces dissipate. But although the number of pieces of direct evidence about what happened may not increase, more and more evidence can be obtained about the reliability of the evidence which we have. One could show the evidence yielded by traces of certain types, or testimony given by witnesses of such-and-such character in such-and-such circumstances was always correct. This indirect evidence could mount up in just the way in which the evidence of the physical impossibility of an event could mount up. Hence by his examining the reliability of the direct evidence, the truth of the 'historical' proposition like the 'scientific' can also 'be tested at any time by any person'.

But if Flew's justification of his principle is mistaken, what can we say positively for or against the principle itself? Now I would urge that it is an unreasonable principle since claims that some formula L is a law of nature, and claims that apparent memory, testimony or traces of certain types are to be relied on are claims established ultimately in a similar kind of way (not exactly the same kind of way – a difference is discussed in note 1 to page 44) and will be strong or weak for the same reasons, and so neither ought to take automatic preference over the other. To make the supposition that they are to be treated differently is to introduce a complicating *ad hoc* prodecure for assessing evidence. As we have seen, formulae about how events succeed each other are shown to be laws of nature by the fact that they provide the most simple and coherent account of a large number of observed data. Likewise testimony given by certain kinds of people or traces of certain kinds are established as reliable by well-established correlations between present and past phenomena. (The reliability of apparent memory could also be assessed in the same way but we will ignore this for the moment, as important only for the few who claim to have observed miracles.) The reliability of C_{14} dating is established by showing that the postulated correlation between the proportion of C_{14} in artefacts and their age since manufacture clearly established by other methods holds of the large number of cases studied without exception and is the simplest correlation that does. That testimony given by Jones on oath is to be relied on is to be established by showing that whatever Jones said on oath is often by other methods shown to be true and never shown to be false, and there is no other simple account of the matter coherent with the data than that Jones tells the truth on oath (e.g. the account that in each of these cases he told the truth because he knew that a lie could be detected).

So then a claim that a formula L is a law of nature and a claim that testimony or trace of a certain type is reliable are established in basically the same way – by showing that certain formulae connect observed data in a simple coherent way. This

43

being so, whether we take the evidence of an established law of nature that E did not occur or the evidence of trace or testimony that it did would seem to be a matter of the firmness with which the law, if reliable, forbids and the firmness with which the trace or testimony, if reliable, establishes the occurrence of E, and of the reliability of each. If the law is universal, it will firmly rule out an exception; if it is statistical, it will merely show an exception to be highly improbable. (On our understanding – see Chapter 3 – whatever, given a statistical law, is highly improbable is considered an exception to it.) Likewise traces or testimony may, in virtue of the correlation used, either show to be certain or show to be highly probable the event in question.

If the correlation between (e.g.) testimony of a certain kind of witness and the past event testified to is statistical (e.g. 'witnesses of such and such a type are reliable in 99% cases') then it shows that the event in question (what the witness reported) having happened is highly probable. If the correlation is universal ('witnesses of such and such a type are invariably reliable') then it makes certain the occurrence of the event in question (viz. given the truth of the correlation, it is then certain that the event happened). So whether the evidence on balance supports or opposes the occurrence of E is firstly a matter of whether the law or correlation in question is universal or statistical in form. It is secondly a matter of how well established the law or correlation is: a statistical law may have very strong evidence in its favour. The basic laws of Quantum Theory are statistical in form but the evidence in their favour is enormously strong. On the other hand, some universal laws are, though established, not very strongly established. Such are, for example, many of the generalisations of biology or anthropology. If L is a law, universal or statistical, to which the occurrence of E would be an exception, and T is a trace or piece of testimony of the occurrence of E, shown to be such by an established correlation C, whether the evidence on balance supports or opposes the occurrence of E is a matter of whether L and C are universal or statistical, and how well established respectively are L and C. (1) If C is universal and better established than L, then, surely, whether L is universal or statistical, the evidence on balance supports the occurrence of E; whereas if L is universal and is better established than C, then, whether C is universal or

44

merely statistical, the evidence is against the occurrence of E. If C and L are both statistical, and C is no less well established than L, and C renders the occurrence of E more probable than L renders it improbable, then the evidence on balance supports the occurrence of E. If C and L are both statistical, and L is no less well established than C, and L renders the occurrence of E more improbable than C renders it probable, then the evidence on balance is against the occurrence of E. What we are to say in other cases depends on whether we can measure quantitatively how well established are C and L and compare these figures with the probability and the improbability which they respectively ascribe to E. How well established or confirmed are L or C is a matter of how well they (or the scientific theory of which they are part) integrate a large number of data into a simple and coherent pattern. Whether one can measure and how to measure quantitatively this degree of confirmation of scientific laws and of generalisations are disputed issues. They are the subject of a branch of philosophy of science known as confirmation theory which has not yet yielded any results of the kind which we could apply to our concern.

In so far as we have several traces or pieces of testimony that E occurred, to that extent the evidence provided by traces and testimony will be very much the weightier. Suppose for example that we have traces or pieces of testimony T_1 and T_2 that E occurred, and that E if it occurred would be an exception to a universal law of nature L. T_1 is evidence that E occurred in virtue of a universal correlation C_1, and T_2 is evidence that E occurred in virtue of a universal correlation C_2. If L is true with no exceptions at all then E did not occur, but (given the existence of T_1 and T_2) if *either* C_1 *or* C_2 is true, then E did occur. It will be more likely that one of C_1 and C_2 is true than that C_1 is true or that C_2 is true. Hence T_1 and T_2 together produce more evidence in favour of E having occurred than does just one of them. It is clearly in virtue of such considerations that the principle of coincident evidence, which I cited earlier, holds. This is the principle that we should not reject coincident evidence that an event E occurred unless the evidence that E did not occur is extremely strong or an explanation can be given of the coincidence. Evidence that E did not occur would be extremely strong if L was very well supported and far better supported than any of the very few correlations $C_1 \ldots C_n$

45

adduced as evidence of the reliability of traces or testimony $T_1 \ldots T_n$ to the occurrence of E. Evidence that the coincident evidence is susceptible of another explanation is evidence of further traces and testimony backed by other correlations $C_{n+1} \ldots C_p$ that exceptional circumstances hold under which $T_1 \ldots T_n$ are not evidence that E occurred. But in general we assume (because $T_1 \ldots T_n$ being traces, it is highly unlikely) or have evidence that those circumstances do not hold.

It is not always easy even to compare the strength of support for various proposed laws or correlations, let alone measure such strength quantitatively. But, as we have seen, laws and correlations are supported in a similar kind of way by instances. Hence it seems reasonable to suppose that in principle the degree of support for any correlation C or disjunction of correlations could exceed the degree of support for any law and hence render it more probable than not that the cited event E occurred. Flew's principle can only be saved if we suppose that support for the C's and support for L are to be treated differently just because of the different role which the C's and L play in supporting or opposing the occurrence of E. But this seems to be to make a complicating, *ad hoc* supposition. Flew's principle advocates treating evidence for generalisations in a different way from the way in which we ordinarily treat it, and is therefore for this reason to be rejected.

It must however be admitted that in general any one correlation C will be less well established than L, and since L will usually be a universal law, its evidence will in general be preferred to that of C. However, the more pieces of evidence there are that E occurred (e.g. the testimony of many independent witnesses), the more such evidence by its cumulative effect will tend to outweigh the counter-evidence of L. This accounts for our previous third subsidiary principle.

Although we do not yet have any exact laws about the reliability of testimony of different kinds, we have considerable empirical information which is not yet precisely formulated. We know that witnesses with axes to grind are less to be relied on than witnesses with no stake in that to which they testify; that primitive people whose upbringing conditions them to expect unusual events are more likely to report the occurrence of unusual events which do not occur than are modern atheists

46

(perhaps too that modern atheists are more likely to deny the occurrence of unusual events which in fact occur in their environment than are primitive people); and so on.

I venture to suggest that generalisations of this kind about the reliability of testimony, although statistical in character, are extremely well established, perhaps better established than many laws of nature. However it must be added that while we can construct wide and narrow generalisations about the reliability of contemporary witnesses which are well confirmed, generalisations about the reliability of past witnesses will be more shaky, for we have less information about them and it is in practice often difficult to obtain more.

Now, although we are in no position yet (if ever we will be) to work out numerically the degree or balance of support for a violation E of a law of nature L having taken place, since *a priori* objections have been overruled, we can surely cite examples where the combined testimony of many witnesses to such an event is in the light of the above considerations to be accepted.

One interesting such example is given by Hume himself:

Thus, suppose, all authors in all languages agree, that, from the first of January 1600, there was a total darkness over the whole earth for eight days: suppose that the tradition of this extraordinary event is still strong and lively among the people: that all travellers, who return from foreign countries, bring us accounts of the same tradition, without the least variation or contradiction: it is evident, that our present philosophers, instead of doubting the fact, ought to receive it as certain, and ought to search for the causes whence it might be derived ([11] pp. 127 f.).

Hume unfortunately spoils this example by going on to suggest that such an event, although extraordinary, is not physically impossible, since

The decay, corruption, and dissolution of nature, is an event rendered provable by so many analogies, that any phenomenon, which seems to have a tendency towards that catastrophe, comes within the reach of human testimony, if that testimony be very extensive and uniform. ([11] p. 128.)

We with our knowledge of natural laws, in particular the laws of meteorology and the Earth's motion, would not judge the matter in this way, but would surely judge the event to be physically impossible. Indeed Hume originally introduced it as an example of 'violations of the usual course of nature, of such a kind as to admit proof from human testimony' ([11] p. 127). (He allowed in theory, it will be remembered, that there could be such, 'though, perhaps, it will be impossible to find any such in all the records of history'.) The example is similar to many which might be artificially constructed in which the amount, diversity and detail of testimony to the occurrence of E surely suffices to overwhelm any information provided by science that E is physically impossible.

The weight of apparent memory

The argument of the preceding pages is that we can assess any testimony or trace of the past on evidence of the reliability of testimony or traces of similar kind. It suggests that we can assess our own apparent memory, or claims to knowledge of our own past experience, by similar tests. It suggests also that any apparent memory of having observed some event E has to be weighed against any other evidence that E did not occur, and that sufficient of the latter could always outweigh the former.

There is an argument against all this by Holland [18] who proposes another principle for assessing evidence, the adoption of which would mean that evidence could on balance easily be favourable to the occurrence of a violation of a law of nature. This is the principle that sometimes evidence of apparent memory is strong enough (quite apart from evidence of its reliability) to outweigh any rival evidence, for sometimes, according to Holland, we can know incorrigibly (viz. in such a way that nothing could count against our claim to knowledge) what we observed on a particular occasion. Holland does not give any rules for distinguishing occasions where we know incorrigibly what happens (whatever science etc. may tell us about what can or cannot happen) – e.g. how long ago our incorrigible knowledge can extend, how familiar we have to be with the subject matter etc. He would probably say that some-times we just do know and realise that we know incorrigibly and that is all there is to it. Holland claims that unless we do say this, 'a distinction gets blurred which is at least as important as the distinction between a law and a hypothesis – namely the distinction between a hypothesis and a fact. The distinction between my saying when I come across an infant who is screaming and writhing and holding his ear 'he's got an abscess' and my making this statement after looking into the ear, whether by means of an instrument or without, and actually seeing, coming across the abscess' ([18] p. 47).

The only argument that I know of to support the claim that we know some truths about the physical world incorrigibly, that some judgements of observations which we report cannot possibly be mistaken, is that given by Holland ([18] p. 47), that 'if there were not things of this kind of which we can be certain we wouldn't be able to be uncertain of anything either'. This argument is given more fully by Norman Malcolm in his 'Knowledge and Certainty' (Prentice-Hall, Englewood Cliffs, N.J., 1963) pp. 66–72. Malcolm claims (p. 69) that 'in order for it to be possible that any statements about physical things should *turn out to be false* it is necessary that some statements about physical things *cannot* turn out to be false'. By 'statements about physical things' Malcolm means empirical statements, statements about the world (as opposed to e.g. statements of mathematics) other than statements about mental states (e.g. the statement that I am now experiencing a pain). I can only consider, he claims, e.g. who did a murder, if there are some physical things about which I cannot be mistaken, e.g. that Jones had blood on his hands. The latter is a fact, the former an hypothesis. Only if there are facts, the argument goes, can I consider hypotheses.

This argument seems mistaken. Certainly for argument, discussion, inference to take place about physical things, there must be some statements about physical things of which we are at present with reason highly confident, and other statements about physical things of which we are more doubtful. Then using the former as premisses, we can discuss the truth of the latter. In this context we treat the former statements as statements of facts and the latter as hypotheses. But all this is quite compatible with the claim that anything taken for granted in one discussion could be seriously questioned in another discussion. In a new discussion what was previously not open to question could be treated as an hypothesis and evidence could be adduced for and against it. A historian may take it for granted in general in discussing ancient history that Trajan became emperor in A.D. 98 but if another historian presents arguments against this assertion, then it in its turn could be discussed. The argument that argument can only take place about physical things and hypotheses about them be rejected if we know some physical things incorrigibly is mistaken.

Given that this particular argument fails, the question remains whether I can ever rightly treat something as a fact if I alone claim to have observed it, its occurrence is apparently physically impossible, and there is no evidence to show the reliability of my memory. My own view is that our standards of evidence are unclear here, that some people would certainly stand by some of their apparent memories despite any amount of counter-evidence and that other people would not and that there are no relevant commonly accepted standards to which members of the two groups can appeal to decide who is right. Thus consider an example of Holland's:

> Suppose that a horse, which has been normally born and reared, and is now deprived of all nourishment (we could be completely certain of this) – suppose that, instead of dying this horse goes on thriving (which is again something we could be completely certain about). A series of thorough examinations reveals no abnormality in the horse's condition: its digestive system is always found to be working and to be at every moment in more or less the state it would have been if the horse had eaten a meal an hour or two before ([18] p. 48).

Now if only one observer is involved, can he really be certain (even without evidence on the reliability of his own memory) that the horse is not being surreptitiously fed? It is not clear, nor is it clear how we can settle whether he can be certain. But if the testimony of others comes in as well as apparent memory (many others claim to have watched the horse in turn day and night), then surely a man can be sure that the horse has not been fed, and so that a law of nature has been violated. (This latter may be Holland's claim in the particular example. Whether he is considering only one observer or many observers

50

who give testimony to each other is unclear from his paper.)

So I conclude that although standards for weighing evidence are not always clear, apparent memory, testimony and traces could sometimes outweigh the evidence of physical impossibility. It is just a question of how much evidence of the former kind we have and how reliable we can show it to have been. However Hume's general point must be admitted, that we should accept the historical evidence, viz. a man's apparent memory, the testimony of others and traces, only if the falsity of the latter would be 'more miraculous', i.e. more improbable 'than the event which he relates'. Subject to a crucial qualification to be considered in Chapter 6, I share Hume's conviction that the balance of evidence is unlikely to be very often of this kind, but the considerations of this chapter indicate, I suggest, that the balance is much more likely to be of this kind than Hume suggests.

5 The Action of a god

So we could have good reason to believe that some event E which occurred was a violation of a law of nature. But for such an event to be a miracle, on Hume's definition, it has to be brought about by a god, that is, a very powerful non-embodied rational agent.

It will be recalled that the third objection in the Humean tradition cited in Chapter 2 was that of Nowell-Smith. Nowell-Smith rightly claims that if a miracle is an event brought about by a god, then we have an explanation of the occurrence of the miracle, the action of the god. He then urges an opponent to consider whether the notion of explanation 'does not involve that of a law or hypothesis capable of predictive expansion. And then let him ask himself whether such explanation would not be natural, in whatever terms it was couched, and how the notion of "the superantural" could play any part in it' ([15] p. 253).

Explanation in terms of purpose or intention

It is important, against this objection, to make a distinction made by many modern philosophers between a scientific explanation of the occurrence of an event and an explanation of the occurrence of an event effected by the act of an agent, that is ordinarily a man, in terms of his purpose or intention in producing it, which I will term personal explanation. These are radically different kinds of explanation. Scientific explanation does indeed involve citing 'a law or hypothesis capable of predictive expansion'. We explain a particular explosion by its cause, the ignition of a particular volume of gunpowder in certain circumstances, in virtue of the universal law that ignited gunpowder in those circumstances always explodes. To cite A, as the cause of B, commits us to a generalisation holding of the form that events of type A are always or almost always followed by events of type B. Any event is, logically, a possible cause of any other. What causes what is a matter of what kinds of events follow other kinds of events.

The explanation however of things brought about by people, that is, of human behaviour, in terms of intention or purpose is explanation of a radically different kind. A purpose or intention in bringing about E is a purpose or intention to bring about thereby some further future state. My intention in going across a road (viz. bringing about the state of me being on the other side of the road) might be to post a letter. My purpose in digging the garden might be to make things grow better next year. A man can only bring about E, having in so doing the purpose or intention to bring about Q, if he believes that the occurrence of E is a step on the way to the occurrence of Q. His purpose in performing a certain action (bringing about some effect) may indeed be inferred from a man's other actions, but it could not be inferred from what normally preceded actions of that type. You could not discover my purpose in going out of the door now by noting what I always or normally did before going out of the door. You might guess my purpose from discovering what I normally did after I went out of the door at about the time of day in question. But mere study of a man's unspoken behaviour will not often tell us a great deal about his purposes or intentions. What he says to others about his purposes and about what he believes will follow what is crucial for the assessment of those purposes. What a man naturally admits to himself about his purposes, and, in so far as he is honest, confesses to others is, in the absence of very strong evidence from his public behaviour, to be taken as the truth about those purposes. If I explain to you my going along some road by saying that my purpose is to go to the shops, this is very strong evidence that that is indeed my purpose. If I do not in the end get to the shops, that counts somewhat against the explanation, but not conclusively – I may have changed my mind. There are various considerations which count for or against my having changed my mind – e.g. it counts for my having changed my mind if I can adduce a reason, which I can reasonably be supposed suddenly to have thought of, which made me change my mind.

The grounds for assessing claims about purposes and

intentions are clearly complex, but what has been said so far should substantiate the claim that explanation by purpose or intention is radically different from scientific explanation. While anything can be a cause in the scientific sense of anything else, if events of the first kind are regularly followed by events of the second, there are other limits described above on what can be a purpose or intention in bringing about some effect. Crucial in assessing what are an agent's purposes are his public utterances – there is no parallel in the scientific case for this.

That there are these crucial differences between scientific and personal explanation has been much argued in writing on the philosophy of mind over the past twenty years. Many of the points have been disputed, but I judge that the consensus of writing gives considerable support to the view stated above. There is unfortunately no space to develop the arguments on this matter further. If these points are at all right it means, against Nowell-Smith, that we can explain the occurrence of an event without subsuming it under laws of nature, and hence that an event could be brought about by an agent, e.g. a god, even if it is a violation of a law of nature. (For some of the main articles in the controversy over the nature of explanation of human action by intention or purpose, and extensive bibliography on the topic, see A. R. White (ed.), 'Philosophy of Action': Oxford University Press, 1968.)

To claim, as I have done, that explanation in terms of purpose or intention is explanation of a different kind from the scientific is not to deny that many events whose production can be explained by the intention or purpose of an agent can also be explained in scientific terms. A movement of my hand may be explained both by my intention to grasp a pen and also by the prior state of my nervous system. I wish only to claim that an explanation of the former type could be correct in cases where there was no explanation of the latter type. Nor do I wish to deny that purposes and intentions are often predictable. Obviously they are – I can often tell what you will intend to achieve in a certain situation. Maybe they could be completely predicted by a man who knew enough about men and their ways. But the point remains that an explanation which cites them in explaining the occurrence of some event is not of the scientific type. (C. D. Broad makes this point in connection with miracles, in somewhat old-fashioned terminology, in [13] p. 90).

But what is evidence that an event E is due to the action of an agent? Let us for the moment consider solely the case of an embodied agent, a human being P. It is normally necessary that parts of P's body (e.g. his hands) bring E about. Normally if P is to be said to have written something, P's hand must have held the pen which made the marks on the paper. I have said 'normally' for telekinesis does not seem logically impossible. In certain circumstances, as we shall see, we might want to say that a man ('just by willing it') made the dice roll a six even though no part of his body effected this result – he did not turn the dice over with his hands or blow on them. But, with one or two odd exceptions, it is a sufficient condition for P having brought about E that the movements of P's body brought about E. One such odd exception where a man's body brings about a result but the man does not is the following: if you take hold of my hand and smash a window with it, my hand has broken the window, but as far as people are concerned, it is you, not I, who have done it. Yet not everything which the movement of a man's body affects, and so normally the man does, does he do intentionally, do, having meant to do. His limbs may move without his controlling them (as in the reflex knee jerk) or the movements of his body produce a result of which he had not thought (as when a man unintentionally knocks over a cup). If an agent P is to be said to have produced an effect intentionally, it has to be an effect which he would admit to having produced (admit to himself, that is, and to others if he admits to them what he admits to himself) and can give a reason for having done (if only the reason 'I wanted to'). If P produces a similar effect intentionally in similar circumstances, that is evidence that he produced the effect intentionally on the first occasion. Another piece of evidence that P produces an effect intentionally is if he produces it in response to a request.

These grounds, if there are sufficient of them well confirmed, could surely sometimes show an effect to be due to the intentional act of an agent, even if the movements of his body did not produce the effect. If the dice rolls with the face upward which any one requests P to produce, but only so long as P is otherwise favourably disposed towards the petitioner, and if P claims to have produced this effect, would we not say that P made the dice roll even if his body did not?

Considerations of these kinds settle an issue whether an embodied agent, e.g. a man, has produced an effect and whether he has produced it intentionally. Now explanation of the personal, as opposed to the scientific type, is, since it is explanation in terms of purpose or intention, only applicable to intentional actions. These are actions which a man does, meaning to do. These alone can he do because he intended or purposed to do something. Since only the intentional action of an agent can be explained in a way other than the scientific, it is with these alone that we shall henceforward be concerned. Now if we show that E was a violation of a natural law, and that P produced E intentionally, then we have shown that P by his intentional action violated a natural law. If E is P levitating or P pushing over a mountain without energy being consumed in the process, and tests of the above kind show that P produced E, meaning to do so, then we can rightly say that P violated a law of nature by his action.

Evidence that a violation is caused by a god

But, on Hume's definition, miracles are wrought by gods, not men. What would be grounds for attributing a violation of a natural law E to the agency of a god? We will continue to suppose that we have no good reason to suppose that there exist (or do not exist) any gods, apart from evidence provided by the occurrence of violations of natural laws. Now we cannot attribute E to the agency of a god on the grounds of having seen his body bring E about, for gods (by our definition) do not in general have bodies. But suppose that E occurs in ways and circumstances otherwise strongly analogous to those in which occur events brought about intentionally by human agents, and that other violations occur in such circumstances. We would then be justified in claiming that E and other such violations are, like effects of human actions, brought about by agents, but agents unlike men in not being material objects. This inference would be justified because, if an analogy between effects is strong enough, we are always justified in postulating slight difference in causes to account for slight difference in effects. Thus if because of its other observable behaviour we say that light is a disturbance in a medium, then the fact that the

57

medium, if it exists, does not, like other media, slow down material bodies passing through it, is not by itself (viz. if there are no other disanalogies) a reason for saying that light is not a disturbance in a medium but only for saying that the medium in which light is a disturbance has the peculiar property of not resisting the passage of material bodies. So if because of very strong similarity between the ways and circumstances of the occurrence of E and other violations of laws of nature to the ways and circumstances in which effects are produced by human agents, we postulate a similar cause – a rational agent – the fact that there are certain disanalogies (viz. we cannot point to the agent, say where his body is) does not mean that our explanation is wrong. It only means that the agent is unlike humans in not having a body. But this move is only justified if the similarities are otherwise strong. Nineteenth-century scientists eventually concluded that for light the similarities were not strong enough to outweigh the dissimilarities and justify postulating the medium with the peculiar property.

Now what similarities in the ways and circumstances of their occurrence could there be between E (and other violations of laws of nature) and the effects of intentional human actions to justify the postulation of similar causes?

Our description of the other grounds for attributing the production of events to the intentional actions of agents suggests grounds of the following kind for postulating similar causes. E occurs in answer to a request (a prayer) addressed to a named individual (e.g. a prayer addressed 'O Apollo' or 'O Allah'). Other such requests are also sometimes granted by the occurrence of violations of laws of nature, but otherwise violations are far less frequent. The making of a request of this kind is often followed by a voice, not being the voice of an embodied agent, giving reasons for granting or refusing the request. These reasons together with the kinds of events produced show a common pattern of character. Thus requests for the relief of suffering might generally be successful, whereas requests for the punishment of enemies might not be. The voice would say to those who asked for the relief of suffering that they had asked wisely, and to those who asked for the punishment of enemies that they were being malicious, and that it was no part of divine providence to forward their malice. All of this would, I urge, suggest a god with a certain character tampering with the

58

world. Normally however the evidence claimed by theists for the occurrence of miracles is not as strong as I have indicated that very strong evidence would be. Violations are sometimes reported as occurring subsequent to prayer for them to occur, and seldom otherwise; but voices giving reasons for answering such a request are rarely reported. Whether in cases where voices are not heard but the occurrence of violations following prayers for their occurrence were well confirmed we would be justified in concluding the existence of a god who brought E about is a matter of whether the analogy is strong enough as it stands. The question of exactly when an analogy is strong enough to render a conclusion based on it sufficiently probable to be believed is always a difficult one and it is hard to give general rules. Yet it is always possible to describe cases where it clearly is and cases where it clearly is not strong enough to render a conclusion credible. I claim to have described a case where the analogy would clearly be strong enough to render credible the conclusion that a god brought about a violation of a law of nature.

Two final points must be made here, one to tidy up the argument and the other to meet a further argument put forward by Hume which I have not previously fully discussed.

Evidence from miracles for the existence of more than one god

The first point is this. Unless we have good reason to do so we ought not to postulate the existence of more than one god but to suppose that the same being is responsible for all miracles. This follows from a basic principle of reasoning that we ought to postulate the existence of no more entities than are sufficient to account for the phenomena to be explained (the principle called 'Ockham's razor' -- *entia non sunt multiplicanda praeter necessitatem*). But there could be good reason to postulate the existence of more than one god, and evidence to this effect could be provided by miracles. One way in which this could happen is that prayers for a certain kind of result, e.g. avoidance of shipwreck, which began 'O, Neptune', were often answered, and also prayers for a different kind of result, e.g. success in love, which began 'O, Venus,' were also often answered, but prayers for a result of the first kind beginning 'O, Venus', and for a result of the second kind beginning 'O, Neptune' were never answered. Evidence for the existence of one god would in general support, not oppose, evidence for the existence of a second one since, by suggesting that there is one rational being other than those whom we can see, it makes more reasonable the supposition of the existence of another one.

Hume's fourth subsidiary argument

The second point, which is connected with the first, is that there is no reason at all to suppose that the fourth of Hume's arguments of part 2 of section x (discussed on pp. 17 ff.) is correct. There is no reason to suppose that Hume is in general right to claim that 'every miracle . . . pretended to have been wrought in any . . . [religion] . . . as its direct scope is to establish the particular system to which it is attributed; so has it the same force, though more indirectly, to overthrow every other system. In destroying a rival system it likewise destroys the credit of those miracles on which that system was established' ([11] pp. 121 f.). If Hume were right to claim that evidence for the miracles of one religion was evidence against the miracles of any other, then indeed evidence for miracles in each would be poor. But in fact evidence for a miracle 'wrought in one religion' is only evidence against the occurrence of a miracle 'wrought in another religion' if the two miracles, if they occurred, would be evidence for propositions of the two religious systems incompatible with each other. It is hard to think of pairs of alleged miracles of this type. If there were evidence for a Roman Catholic miracle which was evidence for the doctrine of transubstantiation and evidence for a Protestant miracle which was evidence against it, here we would have a case of the conflict of evidence which Hume claims occurs generally with alleged miracles. The miracles could be evidence for their respective doctrines in the following way. A devout Roman Catholic priest might be publicly praying to God in church for a miracle to demonstrate the doctrine of transubstantiation when the tabernacle containing the Sacrament levitated. A dedicated Protestant minister might pray publicly for lightning to strike a tabernacle as evidence that the doctrine of transubstantiation was idolatrous, and such lightning might strike it out of a sky

60

empty of clouds without being followed by thunder. Here indeed we would have miracles supporting conflicting claims. But it is enough to give this example to see that most alleged miracles do not give rise to conflicts of this kind. Most alleged miracles, if they occurred as reported, would show at most the power of a god or gods and their concern for the needs of men, and little more specific in the way of doctrine. A miracle wrought in the context of the Hindu religion and one wrought in the context of the Christian religion will not in general tend to show that specific details of their systems are true, but, at most, that there is a god concerned with the needs of those who worship, which is a proposition accepted in both systems.

Fitting our account to other definitions of 'miracle'

So far we have conducted our inquiry into the evidence which can be adduced for or against the occurrence of miracles in terms of the Humean definition of a miracle as a violation of a law of nature by the act of a god. But we saw in Chapter 1 the inadequacies of this definition, and it is now time to fit the account given so far to other definitions.

Firstly, we may wish to widen the Humean definition to allow the agent of a miracle to be not a god but a man. We have described in this chapter the grounds for saying that a man had produced an effect.

Secondly we saw that in order to be a miracle an event has to be in some sense of an extraordinary kind. But this need not, we saw, be a violation of a law of nature; it could be an extraordinary coincidence. If it were such, and occurred entirely in accordance with natural processes, the evidence that a god was responsible for it must be rather different from evidence that a god was responsible for a violation of a law of nature. For a violation of a law of nature is an event separate from other surrounding events, which does not occur in accord with the scientific pattern. Scientifically it is inexplicable. It is to be judged the act of a god according to the circumstances of its occurrence. But an event which occurs in accordance with natural processes already has another explanation. It is explained by natural laws acting on precedent events. Hence if its occurrence is to be explained by something else in a way compatible with that explanation, this can only be because the something else is responsible for the natural laws and the precedent events. The scientific explanation is, *ex hypothesi*, correct. Consequently the explanation by the act of a god is not a rival to this explanation; it can only be true if it is a more fundamental explanation of the scientific explanation. The extraordinary coincidence has the same kind of natural explanation as other natural events, viz. the scientific explanation. Hence the action of a god is only to be accepted as an explanation of the extraordinary coincidence if it is to be accepted as an explanation of all regular natural processes. The action of a god can only explain an extraordinary coincidence within history if it can explain the whole of history as well. The arguments for the existence of a god are almost all arguments for the existence of a god who controls the natural order. Thus the argument from design (or teleological argument) purports to show that the order and succession of things in the world shows a designer and controller. In so far as arguments for the existence of a god together give sufficient support to make credible the claim that there exists a god who controls the natural order, they thereby give sufficient support to make credible the claim that a god was responsible for the extraordinary coincidence. The worth of many arguments, other than the argument from violations of natural laws, to the existence of a god will be considered in other volumes in this series.

Thirdly we noted that the Humean definition was inadequate in not making its religious significance part of the definition of a miracle. We saw in Chapter 1 that there were wider and narrower understandings of religious significance, and we illustrated briefly what these were.

So on the other and more adequate definitions of 'miracle' considerations additional to those involved in the Humean definition have to be taken into account in assessing evidence for or against the occurrence of a miracle. However the major philosophical problems about miracles seem to arise with the notion, involved in most definitions of 'miracle,' of a violation of a law of nature by a god, which is in effect Hume's definition. For this reason I have worked for most of this book with the Humean definition. Now that I have drawn attention to the way in which other considerations are relevant to assessing evidence about miracles in other senses of the term, I shall again work with the Humean defintion for the argument of the final chapter. But the considerations which I shall adduce there will be seen to be crucially relevant to the assessment of evidence for or against the occurrence of a miracle on most definitions.

6 External Evidence

Now so far in the argument we have supposed that there was no other evidence for or against the existence of a god or gods other than historical evidence (evidence of apparent memory, traces and testimony) and scientific evidence (evidence of the regular operation of natural laws), supporting or opposing the occurrence in certain circumstances of violations of laws of nature. We have found in this case what evidence we would need to show the occurrence of violations and how we would need evidence showing their occurrence in circumstances strongly analogous to those in which intentional human actions are performed for us to attribute them to the agency of a god. And I must add that, in my view, such evidence as is currently available about the occurrence of violations and the circumstances of their occurrence is not on balance strong enough to render very probable the interventionist agency of a god. However the case is radically different if we have evidence of other types for or against the existence of a god. I call such evidence the external evidence as opposed to the internal evidence referred to above.

This external evidence Q^1 could join with internal evidence Q concerning the occurrence of violations V of laws of nature in ways analogous to those in which human actions are performed, to support the claim H that at least one god G exists. The greater the support which Q^1 and Q give to H, the more likely it is that if V occurred they were due to the agency of G and so were miracles. Hence the stronger the support which Q^1 gives to H, the less do we require internal evidence Q to show that V occurred in circumstances analogous to those in which intentional human actions are performed in order to attribute them to the agency of a god. For if there exists a being able to produce V (as a god would be), it is natural to attribute them, if otherwise inexplicable, to his agency. Both Q and Q^1 might be insufficient by themselves to render H sufficiently probable to be believed, but together they might do this.

Many Christian theologicans have professed to have this evidence Q^1, evidence stated in the premises of traditional proofs of the existence of God, e.g. the existence of the world, the design of the world, the existence of moral codes, the phenomena of religious experience, the (non-miraculous) history of the world, the history of the Church etc. The worth of many such arguments will be considered in other studies in this series. Although it would be inappropriate for me to comment in this study on the worth of any particular such arguments, one point should be noted. Each argument starts from (in a very wide sense) certain particular phenomena which, it claims, give grounds for belief in the existence of God. Now it may be that although some of these phenomena each give by themselves some support to the proposition 'there is a God', none by itself gives sufficient support to enable a man reasonably to assent to the proposition. However together they might give sufficient support. Similarly, in a scientific case, no one small phenomenon or set of phenomena is by itself going to lend much support to a grandiose scientific theory, yet together many different sets of phenomena often do give enough support to such a theory, to make it probable that it is true. Thus the photoelectric effect, the Compton effect, the stability of atoms, the spectra of hydrogen being governed by Balmer's formula, the distribution of black body radiation etc. together yield considerable support to Quantum Theory, support making it highly probable that the theory is true. Yet each phenomenon by itself lends very little support to Quantum Theory. So the different phenomena which provide grounds for theism may each provide very little support, but taken together very great support. The basic claim of the theist, right or wrong, is that his doctrine 'makes sense' of the whole of his experience, not of various items taken separately. It cannot be emphasised too strongly how misguided is the habit of philosophers of religion of assessing arguments for the existence of God in complete independence from each other. A similar procedure in science would quickly ensure the dismissal of most, if not all, currently held scientific theories.

Evidence Q^1 might not merely support H, the claim that at least one god exists, but a stronger claim H^1 that at least one god exists of a certain character, when beings of that character are liable to intervene in processes to produce certain results under circumstances S, where these results would not otherwise come about. Now if Q and Q^1 together make H^1 credible, there is no heed for Q by itself to be very strong evidence that natural laws have been violated. For if we can show that S is present, miracles are to be expected in view of the character of the god, and H^1 together with very weak historical evidence Q suffices to make their occurrence credible.

Many Christian theologians have claimed to have evidence Q^1 of just this particular type. It would be evidence from the general course of history or from the design of the world or from the existence of moral codes about the character of the god responsible for these things. It would be evidence, say, that he is a compassionate god, or a god concerned that men should know about him. It would thus show that in circumstances S where men were in trouble or ignorant of God and where these states would not be corrected by natural processes, the god was – *ceteris paribus* – liable to intervene in the natural order to remedy these states. (I have written *ceteris paribus* because there might be, indeed, as we shall see, have been, other arguments from history etc. to show the character of God to be such as not to tamper with the scientific order of things, since he is greatly concerned for man to solve his own problems.)

This point was largely (1) taken by the eighteenth-century Christian apologist William Paley (1743–1805) in the 'Prefatory Considerations' to his 'A View of the Evidences of Christianity'. Paley claims that we have other good reasons than historical evidence for miracles giving support to the doctrine of the existence of God and his having such a character as naturally to intervene in the regular order of things. (He set forward these reasons and attempted to show how they supported this doctrine in his later 'Natural Theology'.)

Suppose . . . the world we live in to have had a creator; suppose it to appear from the predominant aim and testimony of the provisions and contrivances observable in the Universe, that the Deity, when he formed it, consulted for the happiness of his sensitive creation; suppose the disposition which dictated this counsel to continue; suppose a part of the creation to have received faculties from their Maker, by which they are capable of rendering a moral obedience to his will, and of voluntarily pursuing any end for which he has designed

67

them . . . suppose it to be of the utmost importance to the subjects of this dispensation to know what is intended for them . . . suppose, nevertheless, almost all the whole race . . . to want this knowledge, and not to be likely, without the aid of a new revelation, to attain it: under these circumstances, is it improbable that a revelation should be made? Is it incredible that God should interpose for such a purpose? . . . Now in what way can a revelation be made, but by miracles? In none which we are able to conceive. [12]

Paley argues that the general course of history shows that God, who is responsible for it, is such as naturally to reveal himself to ignorant and fallen man, that a revelation needs miracles to testify to its authenticity, so that we would, quite apart from the historical evidence, expect to find a revelation surrounded by miracles. Others have argued that the character of God shown from history, and in particular Old Testament history, is such as to expect him to raise once a man, his chosen Messiah, from the dead. That the crucifixion and resurrection of Christ were to be expected is indeed the theme of many New Testament passages (see e.g. the Epistle to the Hebrews *passim* on how man needs redemption from sin, that this must be achieved by the death of a perfect victim, yet the victim, being perfect, must obtain life through his death). Others again have argued from history that God is a God of great compassion concerned with the providential course of history and so such as to intervene in the natural order not only once in a revelation but often, e.g. in order to show his character and keep history on a straight course. If any of these arguments have any weight, we would need only slender historical evidence of certain miracles to have reasonable grounds to believe in their occurrence, just as we need only slender historical evidence to have reasonable grounds for belief in the occurrence of events whose occurrence is rendered probable by natural laws. We take natural laws to show the improbability of violations thereof because they are well-established parts of our overall view of how the world works. But if they are relevant for this reason, then so is any other part of our overall view of how the world works. And if from our study of its operation we conclude that we have evidence for the existence of a God of such a character as to be liable to intervene in the natural order under certain circumstances, the overall world-view gives not a high prior improbability, but a high prior probability to the occurrence of miracles under those circumstances.

Now, as I have stated, it is not the place of this volume to assess the worth of evidence (other than the historical and scientific evidence about violations) for or against the existence of a god of an interventionist character, but only to point out its crucial relevance. If that evidence does favour the existence of such a god, Paley has, to my mind, a conclusive objection to Hume:

> Mr. Hume states the case of miracles to be a contest of opposite improbabilities, that is to say, a question whether it be more improbable than the miracle should be true, or the testimony false: and this I think a fair account of the controversy. But herein I remark a want of argumentative justice, that, in describing the improbability of miracles, he suppresses all those circumstances of extenuation, which result from our knowledge of the existence, power, and disposition of the Deity. [12]

One particular consequence of Paley's argument is that if we already have reason to believe in the existence of a god, the occurrence of a violation of a law of nature E not under circumstances especially similar to those under which human agents often bring about results (e.g. in answer to prayer) could nevertheless sometimes be justifiably attributed to his activity.

We can see this from the case of human actions. The best evidence for a man having done something is that earlier described – it having been effected after the motion of his limbs, etc. But if such evidence for or against a man having brought about an event E is not available, we ascribe some event to his agency if the event is the kind of event which with his character he would naturally have brought about, if he had the power to affect it, if he had the opportunity to effect it, and if no one else with the power and opportunity to do so would have wished to bring it about. We could have learnt about the man's character by seeing what he did under varied circumstances, which need not have included ones closely similar to those under which E occurred. We could have learnt that he was compassionate by finding out that he often gave money to

69

charity, took much trouble in helping those with personal problems who sought his help, had once worked in a leper colony after being moved by the plight of lepers etc. Then in the absence of other evidence we would infer that we would be likely to help someone lying injured in the road. Similarly if a violation of a law of nature E took place, and if the one god of whose existence we have knowledge could and would, from what we know of his character, have wished to bring E about we can reasonably ascribe its occurrence to his action and so term it a miracle.

Thus suppose a faithful blind Christian is suddenly cured in a way that violates natural laws. Then if we have other evidence for the existence of the Christian God (e.g. that provided, if it is provided, by the traditional proofs) and evidence from his other behaviour (viz. what other effects he brought about in the world) that he is a compassionate God and so liable to intervene in the natural order to help the afflicted, particularly the Christian afflicted, then this event can reasonably be ascribed to his intervention whether or not the blind man or other Christians had ever prayed for that result.

However the external evidence might not favour Paley's conclusion. Firstly, it might not lend any support to the claim that there exists at least one god. The traditional arguments for the existence of God might be shown to be worthless, and other arguments produced against the existence of any gods. Secondly, even if the external evidence favoured the existence of at least one god, it might show him to be of a non-interventionist character. More radical Christians have often claimed that God is not the sort to tamper with his divine order. Summarising the views of many such persons (with whom he disagreed), C. S. Lewis wrote that it will 'be felt (and justly) that miracles interrupt the orderly march of events, the steady development of nature according to her own interest, genius or character. That regular march seems to such critics as I have in mind more impressive than any miracle. Looking up (like Lucifer in Meredith's sonnet) at the night sky they feel it almost impious to suppose that God should sometimes unsay what he has once said with such magnificence' ([8] p. 115). Tillich has expressed theological objections of this kind to miracles in the Humean sense:

Miracles cannot be interpreted in terms of a supernatural interference in natural processes. If such an inter-pretation were true, the manifestation of the ground of being would destroy the structure of being; God would be split within himself, as religious dualism has asserted. ([9] p. 129)

Such evidence of the non-existence of any interventionist god would, in advance of any internal evidence, render highly improbable the occurrence of any miracle. Much stronger internal evidence in favour of the occurrence of a miracle than that earlier sketched would be needed to overcome such evidence.

It should by now be apparent that the evidence for or against the occurrence of some particular miracle is extremely wide-spread. With one *Weltanschauung* ('world-view') one rightly does not ask much in the way of detailed historical evidence for a miracle since miracles are the kind of events which one expects to occur in many or certain specific circumstances. The testimony of one witness to an occurrence of the kind of miracle which in its circumstances one would expect to happen should be sufficient to carry conviction, just as we accept the testimony of one witness to a claim that when he let go of a book which he was holding it fell to the ground. With another *Weltanschauung* one rightly asks for a large amount of historical evidence, be-cause of one's general conviction that the world is a certain sort of world, a world without a god and so a world in which miracles do not happen. Which *Weltanschauung* is right is a matter for long argument on matters towards the solution of some of which the other studies of this series offer some sugges-tions. What we have been assessing in this study is the value of the historical and scientific evidence about particular alleged miracles to the claim that a miracle has occurred, against the background of the different *Weltanschauungen*. As we have seen, such particular historical and scientific evidence makes its small contribution to supporting or opposing the different *Weltan-schauungen*.

Notes

Page 2

1. Numbers in square brackets refer to sources listed in the Bibliography.

Page 34

1. The classes must be classes described by what philosophers of science call projectible predicates. That is to say A's and B's must be events of the kind which if we know that they have been correlated in the past, we thereby have reason to believe that they will be correlated in the future. Thus 'fall of barometer' and 'rainy day' are projectible. If a number of falls of barometers have all been followed by rainy days in the past, that is reason to suppose that falls of barometers will be so followed in the future. But if a jule day is defined as 3 June or 18 June or 1 July or 3 July or 4 July, then 'jule day' is not projectible. If the jule days 3 June, 18 June, 1 July, 3 July and 4 July, have all been rainy days this year, that is in itself no reason for supposing that all the jule days next year will be rainy days. The problem of distinguishing between projectible and non-projectible predicates is the problem of which extrapolation is a natural or simple one, discussed in Chapter 3. Philosophers of science have not yet solved the problem of providing a general rule for when a predicate is projectible, but there are obvious clear cases of when predicates are and when they are not projectible.

Page 44

1. C correlates present events of some type with past events of some type and therefore cannot be a scientific law or part of a

scientific theory, because the laws of science are necessarily forward-moving – they show the necessary consequents, not necessary antecedents of some present state. (For argument on this point, see my 'Space and Time' (Macmillan, London, 1968) pp. 167 f. and 177 ff.) It is a consequence of this point that while we can test laws experimentally (viz. by producing an event and seeing whether the predicted event occurs subsequently), we cannot test correlations of the above type in this way. For they correlate a present event with a past event, and we cannot produce an event now in order to make a past event have happened. Yet although scientific laws can be tested experimentally, and correlations of the type in which we are interested can only be tested observationally (viz. by collecting observations), it does not follow that such correlations cannot be established with as great a degree of probability as scientific laws. For the only value of experiments (producing the relevant events ourselves instead of waiting for them to happen) is to secure particularly crucial observations, and there is no reason to suppose that we cannot secure equally crucial observations simply by waiting for them to happen. There may be practical difficulties in securing as good confirmation of correlations of present with past phenomena as of scientific laws, but there seems no reason to suppose that there are logical difficulties.

Page 67

1. Paley showed how external evidence for the existence of an interventionist god could make plausible the occurrence of miracles, but he does not here make the point that the argument can go the other way too. Evidence for the occurrence of violations of laws of nature in circumstances slightly analogous to those in which human actions are performed could make more plausible than before the existence of a god.

74

Bibliography

For classical discussions by Christian theologians of the topic of miracle see:

[1] St Augustine, 'De Civitate Dei', xxi 6–8 and xxii 8–10.

[2] St Thomas Aquinas, 'Summa contra Gentiles', iii, esp. chs 98–103. Translated under the title 'On the Truth of the Catholic Faith' by Vernon J. Bourke (Doubleday, New York, 1956).

[3] Pope Benedict XIV, 'De Servorum Dei Beatificatione et Beatorum Canonizatione, iv: De Miraculis' (Bologna, 1738).

For useful historical discussions of the evolution of the Graceo-Roman and Christian understandings of miracle see:

[4] C. F. D. Moule (ed.), 'Miracles' (Mowbray, London, 1965).

[5] R. M. Grant, 'Miracle and Natural Law in Graeco-Roman and Early Christian Thought' (North Holland, Amsterdam, 1952).

[6] J. A. Hardon, S.J., 'The Concept of Miracle from St. Augustine to Modern Apologetics', in 'Theological Studies', xv (1954) 229–57.

For contrasting modern Protestant theological writing on miracles see:

[7] H. H. Farmer, 'The World and God' (first published 1935; Fontana ed., London, 1963).

[8] C. S. Lewis, 'Miracles' (Bles, London, 1947).

[9] Paul Tillich, 'Systematic Theology', vol. i (Nisbet, London, 1953) pp. 128–31.

[10] Ernst and Marie-Luise Keller, 'Miracles in Dispute' (S.C.M. Press, London, 1969). (This book contains a historical part concerned mainly with extreme liberal Protestant writing of miracles.)

75

For Hume's classical discussion and Paley's answer, see:

[11] David Hume, 'An Enquiry Concerning Human Understanding', section x: 'Of Miracles' (first published 1748; 2nd ed., ed. L. A. Selby-Bigge, Oxford University Press, 1902).

[12] William Paley, 'A View of the Evidences of Christianity' (first published 1794), 'Prefatory Considerations'.

For modern philosophical discussion of miracles see:

[13] C. D. Broad, 'Hume's Theory of the Credibility of Miracles', in 'Proceedings of the Aristotelian Society', n.s. xvii (1916–17) 77–94.

[14] A. E. Taylor, 'Philosophical Studies' (Macmillan, London, 1934). ch. ix: 'David Hume and the Miraculous'.

[15] Patrick Nowell-Smith 'Miracles', in 'Hibbert Journal', xlviii (1950) 354–60. Reprinted in Antony Flew and Alasdair MacIntyre (eds), 'New Essays in Philosophical Theology (S.C.M. Press, London, 1955) pp. 243–53. My page references are to the latter volume.

[16] Antony Flew, 'Hume's Philosophy of Belief' (Routledge & Kegan Paul, London, 1961) ch. viii.

[17] Ninian Smart, 'Philosophers and Religious Truth' (S.C.M. Press, London, 1964) ch. ii: 'Miracles and David Hume'.

[18] R. F. Holland, 'The Miraculous', in 'American Philosophical Quarterly', ii (1965) 43–51.

[19] Antony Flew, 'God and Philosophy' (Hutchinson, London, 1966) ch. vii.

[20] Alastair McKinnon, ' "Miracle" and "Paradox" ', in 'American Philosophical Quarterly', iv (1967) 308–14.

[21] Guy Robinson, 'Miracles', in 'Ratio', ix (1967) 155–66.

[22] Paul Dieti, 'On Miracles', in 'American Philosophical Quarterly', v (1968) 130–4.